Babes in Boyland

Me and my roommate "Iris" during an early snowfall, fall 1975.

Babes in Boyland

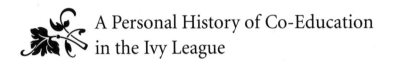 A Personal History of Co-Education
in the Ivy League

GINA BARRECA

UNIVERSITY PRESS OF NEW ENGLAND | *Hanover and London*

University Press of New England

www.upne.com

© 2005 University Press of New England

First University Press of New England paperback edition 2011

All rights reserved

Manufactured in the United States of America

Designed by Katherine B. Kimball

Typeset in Minion by Integrated Publishing Solutions

ISBN for paperback edition: 978-1-61168-203-8

University Press of New England is a member of the Green Press Initiative.
The paper used in this book meets their minimum requirement for recycled paper.

Library of Congress Cataloging-in-Publication Data

Barreca, Regina.
    Babes in boyland : a personal history of co-education in the Ivy League / Gina Barreca.
      p.   cm.
    ISBN 1-58465-299-3 (pbk. : alk. paper)
      1. Barreca, Regina. 2. College students—United States—Biography. 3. Women college
students—United States—Biography. 4. Women in higher education—United States.
5. Dartmouth College—Students—Biography. I. Title.
      LC1757.B37 2005
      378.742'3—dc22   2004024846

5 4 3 2 1

Dedicated with love to "Iris" a.k.a. "Good Times" a.k.a. NBL.

Who knew . . .

This book is called a "personal history" for several reasons, first among them that I've changed names and details in order to save friends, colleagues, and instructors embarrassment. I've combined incidents, conflated experiences, and telescoped the chronology. But the entries from my journals are real, as are the conversations. Real, too, is the particular historical moment framing the book. I remember my years at Dartmouth with a combination of pride, astonishment, and affection. Of these three emotions, astonishment dominates.

Acknowledgments

To Phyllis Deutsch goes all the credit and none of the blame for turning my vague idea about a book on co-education into what has become *Babes in Boyland*. Her enthusiasm for the idea—coupled with her remarkably astute skills as an editor—transformed a dozen notebooks into a manuscript.

To Nancy Lager, Pam Katz, and Tim Taylor go sincere apologies and enormous love, in equal measures, for being the best of friends for almost thirty years. That they acknowledge me on the street is amazing, given their experience of my rococo emotional life. They listened, cajoled, deplored, cheered, forgave, and encouraged in precisely the right ways. I stole their stories shamelessly and changed their names, but they know the truth. Bonnie Januszewski, John Bussey, and Brenda Gross also admit they know me, which is really good.

Rose Quiello wasn't kidding when she suggested that I take my early stories and turn them into something real: the first of my computer files for this project are in folders called "Story for Rose." Catherine Conant, storyteller extraordinaire, helped me construct a framework for the narrative.

To Bob Sullivan and Jay Heinrich go my deepest thanks for giving me permission to embrace Dartmouth as a grown-up. Bob and I met at Dartmouth, true, but only years after we'd both graduated. He was a real D'mouth guy and yet we became true friends almost instantly, which meant that I was forced to reconsider my perspectives on real D'mouth guys. Bob read a lot of this writing in earlier stages—and he inspired some of it. As editor of the *Dartmouth Alumni Magazine,* Jay invited me to use humor in addressing long-standing issues; many of these chapters started as pieces in *DAM* under Jay's wise and provocative editorship. Brooks Clark, a buddy from the Schmooze on the Lake, was generous enough to grant permission to reprint his perfect parody/poem.

To my graduate assistants Mara Reisman, Barbara Campbell, Karen Renner, and Margaret Mitchell go limitless thanks. They did the hard parts: typing from crumbling and yellowed notebooks, organizing, researching, proof-reading—every thankless task was theirs, with years of take-out Indian-food lunches from Wings Express as the only fun part of their scanty recompense. Lindsey Keefe, my undergraduate assistant, read the whole manuscript in one afternoon while sitting on the floor; she, too, is terrific.

To these I also give heartfelt thanks: the members of an organizing committee daring enough to invite me to be the dinner speaker at the twentieth reunion of the class of 1979, where I had a blast and told most of these stories to welcoming waves of laughter, which frankly shocked me; Professor Donald Pease, who gave me my first official invitation to speak as a feminist scholar at Dartmouth; Dr. Richard Scaldini, now President of Hiram College, who gave me that C+; Professors Faith Dunne, Blanche Gelfant, and Mary Kelley for their inspiration; editors of publications where earlier versions of some of these writings first appeared, including the *Chicago Tribune,* the *Chronicle of Higher Education,* the *Dartmouth Alumni Magazine,* and the *Hartford Courant;* my friends, students, and colleagues at the English Department of the University of Connecticut, where I have been fortunate enough to teach since 1987.

To my father and brother, applause, love, and thanks; to the memory of my mother, a gin-and-tonic toast, and curtsey.

And to my husband Michael Meyer, I want to say this: You know you got it, babe, if it makes you feel good.

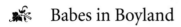 Babes in Boyland

1.

If I could have talked my high school boyfriend into marrying me I would not have gone to college.

I couldn't comfort myself that he wasn't the marrying kind, either. He got hitched right after his freshmen year to the perky girl he'd taken to the senior prom. Perkiness was a quality I was low on in those days. She was skinny, with big blue eyes and an upturned nose. Of course he married her; she was Barbie.

I was Betty Boop. Betty Boop did not have a wedding dress. She had a black garter strapped across her thigh and an annoying voice. Which pretty much summed *me* up on a good day.

If I'd managed to get married, I could have saved myself a lot of trouble. I would not have worried about being the only person at Dartmouth whose last name ended in a vowel (except for Michael Corleone and he was fictional). I could have skipped torturing myself for having lousy skin in a world composed of flawless porcelain. I wouldn't have felt bad having a blanket of dark curly hair when everybody else in Hanover looked like an extra at a casting call for a "Sun-In" hair-lightening commercial. It was clear that the blondes sauntering across campus were real blondes, girls for whom—as they laughed in the old neighborhood—"the drapes and the carpet matched."

Had I married the boyfriend, maybe I wouldn't have been jittery about having to explain that vulgar joke to somebody who pretended not to get it. Or, worse, explaining it to somebody who *genuinely didn't get it* and looked at me as if I were from another planet.

If only it had been me tripping down that aisle into the arms of safe destiny to the strains of Captain and Tennielle's "Love Will Keep Us Together"! I would never again have had to worry about being five points below a curve, ten pounds overweight, or a hundred times too Brooklyn. If I'd gotten married, I wouldn't have had to worry about being exposed as a fraud. As an impostor. As part of some weird experiment. Maybe I wouldn't have been as nervous as an outlaw: a desperado breaking *into* the joint instead of out of it.

Plus with a wedding, you get to choose a band.

Matrimony and education were equally terrifying propositions, yes. But at least other people in my family had gotten married, even if they didn't stay that way.

Nobody—no girl, especially—had gone to college. And if she did, what would happen to such a girl? Who would choose her, the barbarian: perpetually out of place, living half in chaos and half in her heart, when tidier, easier, more acceptable alternatives presented themselves? Guys would run away so fast they'd leave skid marks.

Or so I thought.

And if you thought a very personal history written by a feminist professor concerning the early years of coeducation in the Ivy League would *not* begin with a discussion of lost love, body image, marriage possibilities, skin type, hair color, envy, fear, and boys, then you know nothing about women.

Freshman book photo.

   2.

Janis Joplin, patron saint of every girl who ended up with a guy because he couldn't get the girl he *really* wanted, was singing "Take Another Little Piece of My Heart Now, Baby" as I walked onto the Dartmouth campus in the hot late-autumn afternoon in September of 1975. It would remain my anthem. When I left on a Greyhound bus out of White River Junction in December of 1978, completing my degree in Hanover a couple of terms before our class would officially graduate, I was still whistling the refrain.

"Take Another Little Piece of My Heart Now, Baby" is a bet, a dare—a challenge. C'mon, give me your worst, Joplin invites, because I can take it; don't worry about me, baby, because I can deal with what you can dish out.

Terrific feminist theme song, huh?

The song has stayed in my head all these years because a bet, dare, and challenge is precisely what Dartmouth College was in 1975. At least for women, or at least for working class women, or at least for short, curly-haired women who looked more like Janis Joplin than Farrah Fawcett (whose ubiquitous nipples greeted us from a poster in every guy's dorm room). Okay, so maybe there weren't all that many students who fit that description—okay, maybe I was it—but one thing I've learned after twenty-five years is that all the people I assumed were consummate insiders also felt like outsiders.

The best part of getting older is learning that we have more in common than we ever wanted to admit.

So.

1975 was, among other things, the time when the last of the old male bastion colleges and universities faced the fact that they had to (groan) go coed, whatever the consequences—even if it meant having actual females on campus. Thinking that maybe nobody would notice if they only let women in *a few at a time,* the wisdom of the trustees dictated that we be introduced into the environment slowly so that indigenous life forms had time to adapt. This was also the pre-AIDS era of women's liberation, when sex with strangers did not yet carry a possible death penalty. The only thing that sexual experience slightly affected was one's marriageability—and that was only to certain types of men.

Besides, nobody—male or female—went to Dartmouth thinking, "Oh, this will be a GREAT place to find a mate in an uncomplicated manner." Not with those "Better Dead Than Coed" banners fluttering across Fraternity Row in the warm September breeze, newly painted even though women had been admitted to the college several years before the class of '79 arrived. Not with the guys holding up signs on the balconies in front of the Mass dorms, grading the girls who walked to Thayer for dinner on a scale of 1 to 10, as if three years at an all-male prep school made you into a judge for the Miss America contest. To be fair, with a lot of female students looking toward the faculty for our dalliances, or at least toward upper classmen for our diversions, social life was complicated indeed.

I tried to fit in. Really, I did. I didn't wear my high-heels, at least not during mud season; I traded tight black jeans for gray corduroy pants even though the corduroy made that weird "schwoosh, schwoosh" sound when I walked. I even—and this is hard to admit without cringing—braided my hair. I tried to pass for what I wasn't. I worried that if my peers discovered the scared and scarred girl under all that eye makeup (which no other girl in Hanover seemed to need), they would reject me. The place would disown me. I'd have to become somebody it was exhausting to be: a tough cookie who spent her time singing, taunting, proving "Didn't I show you, baby, that a woman can be tough?"

Being a woman at Dartmouth College in the 1970s was like having a double major. You were not only a freshman, you were also a "co-ed." You were not only a physics major or a government major, you were a "female" physics or government major—as if more estrogen in your system changed everything. More and less was expected of you: You had to prove yourself worthy of the college, but because a punishing rhetoric (often disguised as playfulness) presumed success was impossible unless you were given a head start, your achievements were also often dismissed. You were graded not only by your professors, but also by the boys on Fraternity Row.

Aged alumni as well as freshman boys told you that "The College never should have admitted women. When my grandfather went here, there were no women." You learned to answer "Hey, when your grandfather went here there were also no indoor lights. Sometimes things get better."

You were asked "Are you a lesbian?" because "Only a lesbian would want to go to a men's college," to which you learned to reply, "If I were a lesbian, sweetheart, don't you think I'd have gone to a *women's* college? Would you like me to do the math for you?" (Or perhaps, when asked if you were a lesbian, you learned to answer with an unblinking little smile, "Are you my alternative?")

You learned, in other words, to undermine grim, tight-lipped, earnest, and inflexible all-male traditionalism by being a tough cookie, by being a wiseguy, by being a feminist.

Women at Dartmouth and similar institutions had to learn the rules and play by them in order to figure out how to change them. We knew they needed changing as much as the college song, "Men of Dartmouth," needed lyrics that acknowledged our existence. ("Men of Dartmouth give a rouse/for the college on the hill/For the Lone Pine above her/And the loyal sons who love her/Give a rouse, give a rouse, with a will!/ For the sons of old Dartmouth" etc.)

We learned quickly, as part of a very small community within a larger, older, more entrenched community, how to find our voices and find ourselves—and how to speak up and make trouble. We learned what it feels like to fail and lose—and how it feels to succeed and triumph.

In other words, we learned exactly what girls and women are still learning today: how to challenge institutions of power from within and how to invent a site for yourself even when no blueprint exists for you inside a granite-hard establishment.

And isn't it terrific that some of us, more grown up now, maybe wiser, more successful, and less nervous about how others will judge us, have been privileged enough to enjoy the last laugh?

You know you got it, child, if it makes you feel good.

 3.

"College" was a concept I patched together from an early and illicit reading of Mary McCarthy's *The Group,* from the beach-blanket flick *Where the Boys Are,* and from seeing Sandra Dee in a movie called, as I remember, *Tammy and the Professor.* I didn't fully realize that "college" was as foreign to my family as a camping trip or a welcome call from a government official.

 4.

I was certain that I only got into college because they thought I was somebody else. They must have thought I was smarter and more exotic; surely they thought I was more talented and more original; they most certainly thought I was cuter and nicer and sweeter and better. What they got was me.

Yet I couldn't have told you who that "me" was, at eighteen, because I didn't know.

Even now I can't tell you quite what I looked like back then. I was always trying to catch myself unawares, sneaking a look at my reflection in a bus window or the polished metal of a storefront. Or I'd stare at myself during those long evenings when, for one reason or another, I'd wail the way only a teenager can.

Why did I always look in mirrors when I cried? What is it about seeing my face red and wet that compelled me to look? There's something furtive about it; there's something sneaky, like listening through the walls to other people having sex. The harder I cried, the more I was drawn to any reflective surface. I've spent entire bus and train rides looking at my miserable self in the window—not so that someone else would see me and take pity; that would have been logical—but because I was fascinated. My ordinary non-crying self did not compel me the same way at all—I'd put on my makeup, check my teeth for lipstick, and go—but when I was sobbing, I could hardly bear to look away. It was no less real for all my observation. The rawness of it, the stretched features, the mouth open, eyes reddened. It wasn't pretty. I would sit in front of the mirror and studiously scan my face, searching for flaws the way a copyeditor searches for stray commas and misspellings. I spent time looking in the mirror, but it never helped me picture myself.

Of course, there *are* documents.

In my high school picture, the one included in what was known as The Pig Book (a.k.a. *The Freshman Book,* a compilation of photographs, home addresses, dorm addresses, and school names of every member of the entering class), I'm smiling. That much I know. I'm glancing provocatively over a hippie-style, lace-covered shoulder, hair temporarily calmed down through the judicious application of Tame: the photograph is great.

I looked pretty fetching in a sleazy, barmaid way. The bored photographer who clicked a thousand-plus pictures of our senior class obviously had ideas about a certain type of girl: those of us with long dark hair were positioned looking slanty-eyed and flexible over our shoulders. If you look at the 1975 Oceanside High School yearbook, you'll see nine hundred and fifty normal kids plus fifty who look like they're mail-order brides.

Too bad the photograph didn't really look like me. They airbrushed my skin so that you'd never have thought I burnt myself with a sun lamp or scrubbed my face raw; the caps on two front teeth I got knocked out at a party when I was fifteen were shaded by the photographer and provided a Cheshire-cat grin. The girl in the picture is self-assured, engaging, and fearless. She's everything I didn't think I could ever be.

The other girls at college didn't look like me or my girlfriends from high school. When my friends and I were barely teenagers, we used to walk around town in cutoffs and tight T-shirts offering serious cleavage. We counted how many horns beeped at us, how many whistles screeched, and what sorts of proposals were flung in our collective direction, giving ourselves extra points if guys who noticed us were already with women. It counted more if they already had a girl in the car, although nobody understood why. Let me describe to you one photograph of a bunch of us: we are wearing peasant dresses, popular at the time, and we look, well, like peasants. We do not look like the willowy and romantic girls from *Seventeen* magazine; we look like we just *crossed the border illegally.* I looked like I should be picking escarole from the field with a scarf over my head and a basket tied to my back.

We are wearing gigantic, ugly platform shoes rumored to make your ankles look smaller, meaning we look like peasants who crossed the border from the moon wearing antigravity devices on our feet as we confidently clomp our way into the future. We are all wearing lots of blue eye shadow and I need not say any more about *that,* do I? We have all attempted to press, roll, force, and bribe our hair into long, smooth, silky tresses with hilarious results; if I looked unnatural in my senior picture, in this photograph my pals and I look, collectively, like cross-dressers.

We thought—can you imagine the self-deception involved?—we looked dreamy, intriguing, and slightly mysterious. What we actually looked like makes Jodi Foster in *Taxi Driver* seem as if she stepped out of *Vogue*. We looked like we should be dancing in cages. We wore black liquid eyeliner; we wore Hungry Red lipstick and not to appease our own appetites. I applied makeup with all the subtlety of a child discovering Magic Markers. With a wiseguy grin I perfected early on, I looked exactly like I came from where I came from: a working-class neighborhood on the outskirts of a big city.

I looked like every other girl I knew: sort of trashy, sort of showy, and very, very young despite my desire to appear as a woman of the world.

We thought we looked great.

What did the other female students at Dartmouth look like in 1975? Like Grace Kelly and Gwyneth Paltrow. Like people named after the buildings on campus, or like people who had the buildings named after them. Which they were. One girl had the same name as the dining hall.

That wasn't as funny as the fact that I once met a guy who had the same name as another Ivy League school. Here is the transcript of an exchange I had while trying to make polite conversation with him at a party:

Gina: "Your first name is Yale? Does your family have a connection to the college?"
Yale: "Geeee . . . What do *you* think?"
Gina: "I think it's good your family didn't go to SUNY Purchase."

He didn't think it was funny.

Let me establish a premise concerning the lovely young men at Dartmouth. Individually the guys were like Labrador puppies: jovial, harmless, playful, and cute. They did everything but pee on the fire hydrants.

But no matter how cute the puppies, if you put 2,500 of them together you get a mess.

And the young women?

Many of the other women admitted to the college in the mid-1970s didn't look like women or girls exactly, but rather like hybridized creatures somewhere in between. They were the uber-coeds, drifting across campus with their pale blond hair gleaming like Saran Wrap in the moonlight, wearing their Talbots, their Laura Ashley, their Fair Isle sweaters, and their L.L. Bean. They never raised their carefully modulated voices. Perched on their family money as solidly as hens on eggs, they giggled or glowed but never gaped and guffawed. Trying, perhaps, only to be nice and make a connection, one Talbot girl told me that her parents took her to a special college counselor so she could decide where to go to college. When I offered in response that my cousin had taken me to a psychic on Columbus Avenue for the same advice, she didn't laugh. I was kidding. She thought I was serious. She and the guy from Yale would have really hit it off.

I was intimidated by what I saw as the cool, confident attitude of many other girls in the class of 1979. They always seemed to know the rules: they knew the right thing to wear, understood the right thing to say, and always figured out the right thing to do. They were boxed up and shipped off from their hometowns and small cities and big states, parceled out by their families. They had traveled as if on a package tour, from boarding school or private day school or country day school to Dartmouth. They were a unit, a flock, a herd. They dissolved their individuality as easily as a fish disappears into a school.

I was sure they judged me as an intruder. They must, I thought, see me as a novelty act. To know they belonged, you didn't even have to ask to see their c.v.; you could just check their DNA. My assessment of them was harsh. I could only imagine that their vision of me was even less flattering.

The truth is, I would have loved to look like them. But everything about me was bigger, louder, and more conspicuous. I might have tried to blend in, but it was clear to me, and probably everyone else, that I only succeeded in looking like a duck in a swan suit. (Actually, my brother once said that if I ever tried ballet they'd have to change the name of the piece from "Swan Lake" to "Duck Pond.") I laughed with my mouth wide open, and demanded the place at the front of the line. I inhabited the Lower East Side of emotional life: messy, loud, and confusing to outsiders.

I fought back by necessity—wearing thrift-shop clothes, cowboy boots, tight pants—and anything else that reminded people that I was simply never going to be a "co" anything.

5.

I was by myself when the letter arrived saying that I'd been accepted to college. My brother, older by six years and my only sibling, was living in New York and making his way through the labyrinth of a young man's life. My father worked six days a week with his brothers in a grimy, noisy building in the city making bedspreads and curtains.

My mother had died a year earlier, a bad death, of cancer of the bone and the lungs.

*I didn't look like
a Dartmouth girl.*

I told myself that my mom would have been pleased at my acceptance. My mother was a green-eyed blonde who looked more like the
girls of Hanover than I did, a French-Canadian who left school after
the eighth grade to work as a switchboard operator at a big hotel. I
like to think she would have felt the weight of an old grudge eased
aside had she seen me enter Dartmouth. And although I might be
doing her a disservice even to wonder, it remains one of the central
questions of my adult life: not only whether my mother would be
proud of me, but whether she would like who I've become.

I'm not sure.

Weeks before her death at forty-seven, my mother cut herself out
of family photographs. Baby pictures show only babies, no smiling
mother. Children hold onto empty spaces, looking silly and lost.
Scissors move straight through the middle of some: there's my father in front of the house, alone; there's the tree in the backyard full
of flowers with no one underneath it. It is as if she wanted to see,

exactly, how the world would look without her. Cutting through those pictures must have been like opening a vein, the sharp point making a furrow right through the past.

By the end of her illness, she was living like a boarder waiting to be evicted from a rented room; my mother was ready to check out when she did. She taught me that life was not easy, but neglected to teach me about the magnificence of the everyday. Those lessons I learned elsewhere.

What I remember from growing up was that when I came home from school in the afternoons my mother would be drinking Metracal with an expression of twinned despair and abandon, looking like Hamlet's mother drinking from the poisoned chalice. I thought she was old. She wasn't. My mother would blow Kent smoke out the side of her mouth and lift her head slightly to one side in an unofficial signal of longing and as an intimation of her unquiet life. The small, green, tangled box of a backyard offered her Brooklyn birds and trees; these transfixed her so that she spent much of the day sitting by the window, drinking sweet black coffee, tapping her savagely bitten fingernails on the Formica table top. When she spoke of her youth, she kept looking at the window as if there were a screen with winter scene projected onto it. I looked out, too, searching for her vision and hoping against hope to find myself in it, but I could see only fat robins and bitter sparrows sitting on branches of crab apple, dogwood, and pear.

She grew up in the ferocious wilds of northern Quebec, above Chicoutimi, where she shot rabbits for dinner with a .22 and where her Montagnai Indian grandmother lived happily in a tar-paper shack. This feral grandmother took up with a new man every year despite, or perhaps because of, the arctic temperatures, the lonely forests, and the family's pervasive sense of unexplained exile. Scandalous and happy, the grandmother gave her sons away to be raised by families in the villages who did not have enough children of their own. But she kept a hold over their imaginations, and her birth children circled around her like a wagon train when she died, remembering only that they loved her—not that she had given them away.

Outraged on his behalf for his infant abandonment, my mother tried to get my grandpa to admit his plight. But my grandfather didn't care at all. He carried a photograph of his mother with him until the day he died, folded up in his old man's cracked leather wallet.

So my mother lived her life in translation, raising her children in something besides a mother tongue. In this she was like her own mother, who spoke not French Canadian but a mixture that included native words, ones my mother could no longer recall. She slipped off her mother's language and left it behind, the way a kid loses a pair of homemade mittens. Embarrassed not to be speaking the customary bastardized language of her peers, she didn't know that they were themselves speaking a French no one in France would ever recognize. The words traded in these tribes were a hand-hewn and uncommon currency. What my mother spoke was the language of those who held no right to words they didn't manufacture themselves, just as they had no right to own clothes they didn't sew, or to eat food they themselves didn't cook. You could only own what you made. Everything else was theft or mimicry.

I heard about how her own mother, terrified of thunderstorms, dragged them all out, all seven kids, into the soaking dark and onto soaking wet dirt roads to go to a neighbor's house. Once there they all sat beneath a tin roof listening to the thunder, under the watchful eye of the neighbor's twenty-year-old retarded daughter who stared without blinking into the eyes of children who could have been hers if she'd been born on a happier day or with luckier genes. Sitting in a house with a tin roof to escape fear of a thunderstorm seemed about as safe as sticking a lightning rod into your mouth, but when I heard the story, the only questions I asked my mother were about herself.

"What did you talk about with the neighbors? Did you speak to the weird, scary, tragic daughter?"

"When did your mother decide it was safe to leave?"

What I would ask her now, were she willing to tell the truth, is "Why were you forced to wake up out of a night's calm dreaming just to make certain that you would witness your mother's fear and develop a taste for disaster?" And then I would ask the same question of myself.

The question she liked to hear from me was the one where I asked her to tell me about how she and my father met.

"I met your father at the beach," my mother would tell me. She would be sitting at the kitchen table, smoking, looking out the window. I would be drawing pictures, sitting on my knees to reach the kitchen table, fat crayons in my hand, forming circles carefully on unlined paper. Our enormous orange cat inevitably sat on a corner of the paper, paws like boxing gloves, cramping my margins. This was one story I asked for often and, unless my parents were having a terrible fight, she told it willingly. She would adjust the blue or pink or yellow housedress she buttoned up like a uniformed worker everyday, light a fresh cigarette, and start with the most important part. "We were both reading *From Here to Eternity.* I saw him. Then he looked up and saw me." She had photographs of herself at the beach, long legs for a short woman, big dark movie-star glasses nearly obscuring her small features. Posed.

"I worked all day at the phone company putting through international calls. It was August, hot, and I came home tired. But when my girlfriend Hélène who worked at a dress shop called to invite me to the beach, I just picked up and went. She always got me a good discount and I didn't want to disappoint her. But it wasn't really Hélène calling, even though it was her voice; it was *destiny* on the other end of the line that afternoon. I'd been putting through calls from foreign cities all day but that one time, through Hélène, long distance called me."

I loved that part about destiny. It made me shiver and close my eyes in a tight smile. It wasn't just an accident, their meeting, their marriage, our family. I loved the sense of sweeping purpose behind it. That the beach could be a place for a chance—but still providential—collision of human beings, that such a frivolous place could be the geographic location for the seriousness of my parents' first encounter, awed me. I learned not to discount the apparently random invitation.

And for the next thirty-five years I always ran to answer the phone.

It was August 1946. My father had returned from the war, still surprised to wake up every day, fresh from bombing Europe. He'd been the radio man on a Liberator bomber, his fingertips alive to sounds and pulses in the silent hollow plane. He had spent two years making calls to longer distances with shorter messages than the one that went through my mother. My mother patched through calls with people crying or gossiping; the messages transmitted to my father came with numbers and pinpoint locations. They were both—my parents—receivers, conduits, channels. They were used by others to get the point across.

Words, like oxygen, were passed through tubes and wires known to my father but unfamiliar elsewhere. Words would fall like pebbles bouncing off the metal walls in the bomber, so nobody spoke. Not even the man with the mouthpiece. This was different from his seven-sistered house on Ocean Avenue in Brooklyn where everyone spoke simultaneously and at all times. His all-male, all-silent nighttime world would be sealed shut after the bombs fell on Japan. He signed off his days of signaling, relieved. He wasn't like other men who loved the sharp cold sense of war's importance. He didn't speak about his wartime life until thirty years after it was over, when we faced each other over a cold dinner the week after my mother died and I asked him for the first time about his youth.

He told me parts of their courtship story that my mother hadn't mentioned to me. When he drove the back roads to Quebec with a friend from New Jersey who had a Canadian cousin, there was not even a radio in the Buick. There were just two regular guys, getting away from the families that had no idea of what they'd just seen and done for two years and so treated them as if they had never left. My father worked in a plastics factory; his friend spent nine hours a day in a chemical one. They didn't talk about where they had been. They didn't talk about what they were doing, or their families, or their girls. They talked about where they were going, and that was a strip of rocky beach up north.

Who knows whether my mother and father were both reading books that day, or whether they were simply part of the heat and water and lushness of an uncertain Canadian summer? He'd enough of Bayridge girls in shiny dresses with starched black curls and snapping gum. She rejected the chipped-toothed boys who flocked around her mother's boarding house, calling them "pieces of men." My father's New York voice scratched at her heart like a penknife, leaving his initials there.

She sent him letters full of perfectly quoted lines from the American movies she went to almost nightly to improve her English, letters he kept hidden from his mother and relatives who could barely read but who nevertheless would understand that my father's real life was elsewhere. "We will always have Montreal," she wrote him, and surely she pictured herself as Ingrid Bergman in gauzy black and white? She kept none of his letters, which were brief and full of nothing but information. They had long illegal conversations on stolen telephone company time.

Before she met my father, I know that she had loved one boy deeply, passionately: an engineering student who left for a year and never once wrote. He showed up the next autumn at her door, but she had already met my father. Of the engineering student my mother would tell me, "Remember that you'll have a lot of time to sit and think when you are no longer young about what you did when you were young. What you do stays with you always even after you stop doing it," and "It is not enough that somebody loves you if he leaves." My father also left but returned sooner than the other one. So he won. Whatever else he did, my father never left for good.

My mother never got the chronology right. Whichever way I did the math, I could never figure out how long they courted before they married and had my brother. They saw one another on weekends, with my father driving more than five hundred miles of lousy black-top and asphalt through hellish little towns in upstate New York that frightened him more than the bombed-out villages he'd passed through in Italy. Both my parents were terrified beyond reason of small towns and rural life. But he drove those miles after a full work week for a couple of years to go see a blond girl with green eyes. Once he called from a motel in Mechanicsville because the muffler fell off his car and he was waiting for a part. My mother cried so hard, he said, that instead of waiting he took a bus, spent eight hours with her, took the bus back to Mechanicsville, and then drove home.

They never celebrated their anniversary, and there were no photographs of a wedding even though there were photographs of many other occasions, including ones of my mother's father in his casket right before his burial, taken under a bright flash of blue light that made him look unappealing even for a corpse. I wondered if there *was* a wedding but twenty years after her death my father explained that, in fact, there had been not only one ceremony, but two. He didn't say why, but he confessed that they were married in New York's City Hall and also in the vestibule of a Catholic church in Quebec City where there was a brief ceremony in French.

I remembered a laughing conversation my parents had one day when my mother was starting to be really, irreversibly sick. She was reminding him, with half a smile, that he had promised to stay beside her in sickness and in health. He interrupted her, declaring that because the whole thing was done in a language he couldn't understand, he had no idea of what he promised. "You dragged me into that place and told me to say 'Oui' every time the priest paused and looked at me. I was terrified. I had no idea of what I was swearing to. I just kept saying 'Oui.' I could have been joining the Foreign Legion for all I knew. . . ."

By the time I was maybe fourteen, I figured out that nobody, I don't care how different things were back then, would drive that far and go through that much trouble to see somebody for dinner and a movie and holding hands. I used this secret formula to assuage my own guilt at assignations nearer to home; I never once asked my mother what they had done with their twenty hours every other week. I didn't want to know.

There are almost no pictures of my mother, still fewer of my parents as a couple, and not one—not a single one—of the four of us together.

Yet still I see my mother, in the parking lot with the red and blue market behind her; she smiles at me as I carry the packages. We open the car doors, switch the radio on, and drive away.

*Antoinine Yvette Groulx, circa 1948, on
a beach in Quebec, age 23. My mother.*

*Hugo Barreca, circa 1944, U.S. Army
Air Force, age 21. My father.*

6.

FADE IN:

Gina's BEDROOM IN OCEANSIDE, NEW YORK, a noisy, crowded Long
Island suburb desirable because of its strategic location only three
train stops from Queens. The walls of the small room are painted
bright purple. The ceiling is turquoise. Posters of The Doors and
Jefferson Airplane practically cover one wall; another has smaller
posters of Phil Ochs, Joni Mitchell, Simon and Garfunkel, and,
yes, Janis Joplin. The third is filled with posters of the New York

Rangers' hockey team. Around the room are old hats from thrift shops hanging on nails; beaded bags cover the bureau; platform shoes and Frye boots peek out from under the bed; an open can of TaB as well as lots of books (including *Fear of Flying* and *A Tree Grows in Brooklyn*) and cassette tapes bunched on top of a small black and silver tape player eat up all the space on a shaky desk; a surprisingly neatly made bed with an elaborate magenta print spread, made by her father, is pushed against the wall.

Ticket stubs from concerts are taped to a cut-glass mirror, lots of half-opened makeup bottles including a big perfume bottle of Evening in Paris crowd the dresser top. Prominent on the foot of the bed is a lime green nylon jacket emblazoned with the logo of the place her boyfriend works, a towing, recovery, and wrecking joint whose motto is "We Meet By Accident."

Gina, an eighteen-year-old girl, is sitting on the floor next to her bed, fingering an envelope she is clearly afraid to open. She holds it up to the light, trying to read the letter through the envelope, puts it back down, looks at a photograph of her mother. Gina then looks at a statue of the Virgin Mary (which she always turns to face the wall when her boyfriend visits) until finally she tears the envelope open. Ripping the letter by accident, she reads it in glimpses as she frantically pieces it together.

She gets the kind of look on her face you see when lottery winners are presented with their cash.

She bolts upright and runs down two flights of stairs—past the old photographs cheaply framed on the walls, past the living room with the vinyl-covered furniture, and into the kitchen, where she calls her aunts in Brooklyn.

The house she calls is where her grandmother lived, now populated by three late-middle-aged ladies in flower-print housedresses with white collars and aprons. They look for all the world like the fairy godmother in Disney's *Cinderella*.

"I GOT INTO COLLEGE!" Gina screams, waving the letter.

They are silent. This is not news they expect—or necessarily want.

"Yeah? College? Since when are you going to college?" asks Josie, the head aunt.

"*Nobody* goes to college," whispers Carmela, a secondary aunt whose mouth you could *practically hear* turn down in disapproval.

"Yeah, but her mother, she was always big on school, God rest her soul, right?" offers Marie, the third, sotto voce.

"Where you gonna go to college, Gina?" yells Josie, as if talking through a megaphone.

Clearly prepared for this sort of reaction, not expecting them to understand, Gina is not disheartened. She thinks they are worried about who will pay for this escapade.

"It's okay, I got a scholarship to a place called Dartmouth. I gotta work and take out loans, but it'll be great."

"You don't want to go to Kingsborough Community?" Josie suggests, and simultaneously Carmela asks, "So where is this Dartmouth?"

"I wanna go to this college," Gina explains, "It's really good and it's only in New Hampshire, which is like six, maybe seven hours away by bus. Not so far." She nods into the telephone receiver, now expecting a more positive reaction.

There is still silence on the other end of the phone.

"New Hampshire?" drawls Carmela slowly, "You gonna *go to school* in New Hampshire?"

Long pause before she delivers what she knows to be the punch of truth, "You're pregnant, right? Just like your cousin Philomena."

Gina imagines the three aunts shaking their heads in the unison of their grave disappointment.

"No, no! This is a GOOD thing, this is a big deal."

"Who says so?" asks Carmela. "Why do you need an education to make a home and a family? You think it will make you happy?"

"No, Aunt Carm, I think it will make me smart."

Josie says, "You're glad about this? Good. Your mother would have been proud of you."

More silence.

Carm takes the phone into her own hands and yells, kindly, "And you know, when it's all over, this college, whatever, you can always come home." Pause, sigh. "Like Philomena."

Gina figures she has plenty of time to decide whether Dartmouth College is the right place for her. Nobody expects her home for nine months.

🐜 7. *Conversations*

"The dorm cluster I'm assigned to is called 'Choate.'" I pronounce the word with two syllables—the only way I can imagine pronouncing it. "Isn't that funny? Like I'm living 'inchoate'"?

"Huh?"

"Look, here's the letter. I'm in this dorm, Choate, right, so I'm 'inchoate'—you know, like 'partially but not fully existing' or 'incomplete or imperfectly formed.' It was on last year's SAT, I think."

Silence. Then: "You're pronouncing it wrong. It's 'Choate' like the prep school. And your dorm is there."

🐜 8. *Diary Entry: September 1975*

I am sitting here in a pastel cell given me, unwillingly, upon arrival. I am not in one of the dorm rooms that has a fireplace. Maybe they thought I would cook on it. When I went to the housing office, they told me I was supposed to be in a triple. I showed them the letter from their office promising I had a double room. I forced Dad to leave before I embarked on all this wrangling because otherwise he'd have gone fierce about sorting it out.

So I am in a dorm that I thought was a joke.

But like everything I think is a joke here, the name is perfectly serious.

So I dragged two huge suitcases through the grass and onto the tree-lined walkways, with very little idea of where I was going and a grow-

ing awareness of the fact that I didn't need all this junk I brought with me. I needed to jettison this crap. Maybe at some point (yesterday? How could yesterday have happened only yesterday?) I believed it would be useful, but already I know better and it's slowing me down. Every useless item I brought from home (why did I bring a lamp? There's a lamp in the room) I carried about a half a mile to this dorm.

Then I take a non-restful nap and wake up just as it starts to get dark. I am aching toward the telephone in the hallway. I want to call home. There's nothing I need to hear and nothing I want to say, but I want to call home. Did I feel this way at the beginning of high school? Awkward, assuming, loud, and stupid? Maybe, but it sure feels like I'm dealing with it for the first time. I feel like Margaret Mead on her first day among the Samoans. Actually, I feel more like a Samoan among a thousand Margaret Meads.

I just wish I were home watching television.

My room looks like Queens, like a studio apartment in Rego Park. Oh, God in Heaven, please let it be better than this. I expected a learning experience, but I was only kidding about joining a convent. But that's exactly what this green, cinderblock, one-windowed, small room looks like. There are two nun-sized beds ("Why do they call them nuns?" "None of this and none of that." Aunt Tina's favorite joke, ha ha?), a couple of pale wooden desks, not too old, two wooden chairs, and built-in bookshelves next to a closet. The best thing is the window; it's huge. Just in case I thought I was still in one of the five boroughs, I can see that I'm not: everything is green, outside the room as well as inside. Even in the near darkness, the campus practically throbs with greenery.

It's also about 70 degrees and the only clothes I have are for those freezing New Hampshire winters I've heard so much about. Yeah, and the lousy three-piece pinstripe suit I bought because I was afraid people would dress up to go to class. I can tell already that I'll never wear it. Forty bucks down the drain. What else? The grapes I brought have seeds. I've always hated seeded grapes.

I also look like death. This bothers me and I would probably consider my experience here a little less hostile if I thought I looked beautiful. And right now I'd hug anybody with a limp, or a lousy haircut, a cleft palate, or a lazy eye. Anybody not perfect. A person who bites her cuticles, has a lisp, or eats with his mouth open. Male, female, I'm not picky. Anyone human.

I look out my window and see packs of students, blond heads glowing with their own reflected light like enormous fireflies. You could read a book by the whiteness of their teeth. Not quite human as far as I can tell; nobody of woman born looks that good. They must all be from the Planet Pepsodent.

Will I have this paralyzing sense of inadequacy if I make it through college? I am afraid of getting older and scared of being too young. I'm afraid of selling out to get what I want. I am even more profoundly afraid of not getting what I want no matter what I do. When I'm back in the kitchen with Dad and Aunt Josie and the rest, none of this will seem real, right? Maybe that's what scares me the most. That my only reality is that kitchen.

So I have to learn to be part of this. Why? So I can get a job and not have to get married just to have something to do. So when I do get married it won't be because I have bad dreams or doubt my sanity or because I can't enjoy something without having a witness to validate my pleasure, as if happiness were a parking receipt.

And what do I remember of happiness? What do I want back? I want back that one night, May 12th, with Mr. Cutie-Pie, the social studies teacher. The one night we actually snuck out of our roles and our real lives and went to Jones Beach. The wine was warm in our mouths, the olives bitter; the sausage nipped and teased our lips, heat still came off the salt-smelling rocks. The sand looked like scoops of peach sherbet in the dusk. We sat on a rough wool blanket from the trunk of his car. We talked forever but neither of us made a move; at the end of the evening we walked back to the parking lot holding hands. That was it. He dropped me off in front of the house and said good-night. My memories of him are lighted from behind by all those bridges he told me not to burn.

And so I am in New Hampshire. Maybe it is a trial by fire. Maybe it has to be.

 9.

A freshman year in college is full of trials for a boy; but, for a girl who enters an institution where boys have held undisputed sway for generations, every day brings persecutions which he never feels.

He enters a field which has been his without dispute from time immemorial, for his father and grandfather were there before him; while for her every step costs a battle, and every innocent action is the subject of unkind criticism. She is presupposed to be loud, masculine, and aggressive, until she proves herself different.

... [T]hey were mostly brave, high-minded girls, and hoped to disarm criticism by their daily life and work, rather than by angry retorts, and by degrees they succeeded.*

*From Olive San Louie Anderson, *An American Girl, and her Four Years in a Boys' College*, New York: D. Appleton and Company, 1878.

10.

The green canvas knapsack from the Army Navy store was slung over Gina's left shoulder. It was pulling her head to the left slightly, although she didn't seem to notice, so adamant her step, so directed her walk. The only jewelry she wore was a Timex watch; she wore lipstick and mascara. She walked across campus liked she owned the place.

Until something dark suddenly buzzed across her path.

In one swift gesture, she swung the knapsack in a wide but controlled arc, just missing the creature that buzzed away. "What are you doing?" yelled a male voice from one of the open windows at a nearby dorm.

"A fucking water bug just flew into my face!" she screamed back, her knapsack now at her feet and one hand shielding her eyes from the bright September sun as she looked up to see who belonged to the voice.

"That was not a water bug, you moron, that was a hummingbird!" the voice bellowed. "You almost killed a goddamn hummingbird."

"No way!" She answered automatically, but her stomach flipped over like a cold pancake. It *was* big for a water bug, although she'd seen some big water bugs in her day. She'd never seen a hummingbird; maybe she'd seen exhibitions of them at the Brooklyn botanical gardens but that was it.

But would a hummingbird have made the horrible sawing, buzzing sound she heard when it almost flew into her hair? "No way," she repeated, picking up her knapsack, this time putting both her arms through the straps, pulling her frizzy shawl of hair to one side and then the other as she adjusted the pack on her back.

"What a jerk!" accused the voice, as it turned up the volume on the Grateful Dead's "Sugar Magnolia."

Hello, first day of college.

   11.

She arrives in Hanover to discover that there is more to learn about the college and its traditions—traditions apparently in place since the dawn of man—than she ever could have imagined. She's thrown right into it after she and her roommate, Iris, get invited to a full slate of official and unofficial activities.

Iris and Gina cross the campus, walking past the girls from women's colleges who are getting off buses wearing the blinking, startled look of refugees. Each is helped off the bus as if she is incapable of independent motion and handed a white rose by a neatly dressed young man. The better-looking girls are then abducted by fraternity guys who then escort them, still dazed and wide-eyed, to houses on Frat Row. Presumably each young woman is then deposited in a living room the way a dog might deposit a chew toy.

When one of the guys, suspicious of their motives, asks Gina and Iris why they're hanging around the buses, Iris replies, "We're just browsing, thanks," and they walk off toward the huge pile of wood dominating the center of the Green.

They walk past the site of the bonfire where other, more enthusiastic members of the class of '79 are are stacking railroad ties into the evening sky. ("Whole towns in Canada are now entirely cut off from civilization," Iris observes.) These will be set ablaze as part of a tradition; each incoming class is challenged by upper-division students to stack the highest pile of wood, which they must protect from the upperclassmen who are themselves charged to maintain their own incendiary ascendancy by trying to burn the structure down to the ground before the set date (how could it be fun if nobody risked deep humiliation and loss?).

Iris and Gina go to the quasi-official concert welcoming the freshmen. "Freshman" remains the word used to describe members of the class of 1979, the term "incoming student" being rejected as sounding too much like the cry used by military personnel when under enemy fire—as if you should duck when you see one heading your way—and the phrase "first-year students" being dismissed as sounding too snotty and English. Iris and Gina, being Good Girls—a position they will later reject—sit up front at the concert.

This is a mistake.

The chorus—still virtually all male, maybe four women out of thirty—sings the college songs. The school song, cherished by generations, is not supposed to be funny but it includes a stirring line at which Gina begins to laugh uncontrollably.

When Gina laughs, she is not particularly decorous and subtle. In fact, she does everything but snort and paw the ground. But how could you not laugh at a line describing Dartmouth undergraduates as having "the granite of New Hampshire/ in their muscles and their brains." ("Was this written by somebody who went to Princeton?" Gina sputters. Iris would, at this point, like to shove Gina off the balcony—or at least move away from her on what Arlo Guthrie would have called "the Group W bench.")

Finally Gina calms down and starts breathing normally—having been assessed by the entire audience as scurrilous, although they might have been using words of fewer syllables to describe her—and the chorus sings what is supposed to be a funny parody of another traditional college song. The funny part includes a thinly veiled reference to rape. "Dartmouth's in Town Again, Run, Girls, Run/Dartmouth's in town again, fun girls fun/our pants are steaming hot, we'll give you all we've got. . . ." The chorus seems to be singing directly at her. She tries to make herself laugh, or even smile, but all she feels is her face getting hot.

It's not a good moment.

Suddenly, everybody looks away. If they looked away because a fleet of UFOs landed on top of the Hopkins Center, Gina would still have been relieved. But what happened was even more surprising: an aristocratic-looking girl stands up and reads from a statement declaring the sexist nature of these songs to be unacceptable and she and a small group of other female students walk out in protest.

Gina doesn't move. These girls, sure of their rights, embarrass her.

The event ends. Despite the earlier laughing incident, Gina and Iris are invited to frat parties at different houses, so they make a plan to meet in an hour to check in with each other. Gina heads toward a white clapboard house where David Bowie's blasting from the speakers. She's shocked to find the blond girl from the event, the one who gave the feminist speech and walked out, with a beer in her hand and looking entirely at home.

She says something in a familiar tone to the guys who are drinking and swearing good-naturedly, and they back off, still smiling, but eyeing her with combined respect and distaste. "My brother is the president here, if you can believe it," she explains. "And I've been their unofficial mascot since I was sixteen and came to the house for the weekends to escape boarding school. I'm a sophomore now. Nobody gives me any shit; they treat me with kid-sister gloves. I can belch as loud as any of them, I can eat linguini with my hands, I've launched myself into the air to win a game of beer-pong, and I've beaten most of them at poker."

She describes her flight to Lebanon Regional Airport earlier in the day: "I was in a twenty-seater prop-plane, strapped in beside a man three times my size who kept making noises indicating that he desperately needed to spit. Clearly he was attempting to refrain from spitting in order to act gentlemanly. This means we both spent one hour and forty-five minutes concentrating on his *phlegm*. I considered offering him one of my monogrammed handkerchiefs—my mother gets these for me every year even though I only ever lose them—but since I'd done nothing but nod and smile since I sat down, it seemed—what can I say?—overly *purposive* to ask this suffering soul why he did not accept the relief nature was so clearly trying to offer. Finally I couldn't put up with it a second longer and yelled out, 'For the love of God, man, *just spit*.'" "What happened?" Gina cries. "He got out a Kleenex and did what he should have done hours before. He looked sheepish and I wanted to crawl under the seat and die, to tell you the truth. But at least our ordeal was over and I probably wouldn't have had the guts to say anything if I didn't have four older brothers. Want a beer?"

She introduces herself as "Tiger" and the nickname sounds just right.

Iris at work in our Brown's Hall dorm room.

12. *Conversations*

She was tall, lean, broad-shouldered, and short-haired because she was a swimmer.

"Anybody ever mistake you for a guy?" asked the wit, grinning to see if any of his buddies could share in this moment of triumph.

"No. How about you?" answered Tiger, as she took a sip of her drink.

🐜 13.

My trip to college was different from Tiger's. No airplanes were involved; no embroidered handkerchiefs were considered. My father drove me up to Hanover in our cranky, silver 1967 Buick Skylark, a long trip without air-conditioning but with the country station turned way up. Fear made my spine feel cold, as if somebody were running a fingernail straight down my back. Fear made me sit up straight because God knows I was sitting like a godamned Marine cadet. I believe my father commented on this very point, breaking our conversational silence by barking, "Why you sitting like a godamned Marine cadet, Gina? You practicing for a pole-sitting championship or whatever it is college kids do?"

I was dressed like I was always dressed back in New York—black jean skirt, black T-shirt, black boots, and lots of kohl eyeliner—and I was terrified when I started to see the other students sauntering around campus in chinos and polo shirts. They had their own cars, and on top of these cars they had ski racks. Their back windows provided their curriculum vitae: stickers announced "Loomis Chaffee" or "St. Paul's" or "Brearley."

I was visibly shaken.

A man of few words, my dad said the right thing. Without looking in my direction he observed lightly, "You can always take the next bus home." It was better than magic.

His succinct phrase has been a talisman to me since 1975, because it's given me permission to take risks without worrying about the irrevocable. "I can always take the next bus home," I thought when I moved to Cambridge, England, in 1980 on a Reynold's Fellowship, or when I moved back to New York to start graduate school, or when I moved to Storrs to begin teaching at the University of

Connecticut. Every time I remember that line I think of the airless drive to Hanover, and to the beginning of my life away from home. Beginning at Dartmouth is associated inexorably in my mind with a sense of difference, of fear, and of limitless adventure.

I needed a sense of humor to face early fraternity parties punctuated by beery guys named Skip or Chip asking me where I went to school and then sneering when I replied "I go to school here." It was a year before I added "And where do *you* go?" which at least caught the attention of anyone who might also have trouble with the usual dating rituals.

I can't imagine that freshman year is easy for anyone; surely even the suave and sophisticated amongst us were driven by their own insecurities and worries.

But nothing—no class, no exam—was as hard as social life. Compared to figuring out codes of behavior, lectures and seminars were a piece of sweet cake. It wasn't only girls who found it hard to get a handle on the place; Dartmouth was divided by class as well as by gender. Where you grew up also got factored in.

I remember that one kid in my class first semester came from the town of "North" in South Carolina where, he explained, "It was just hell for anybody to get mail." One day another guy joined our study group and mentioned that he also grew up in South Carolina. "We lived near Four Holes Swamp." A guy who sounded as if he'd never been south of Greenwich smirked, "Is that like a rating system down there? Like a hotel getting two stars or something?"

It wasn't very easy to figure out your role if you didn't have the script.

The book assigned in every first-semester English class was John Milton's *Paradise Lost*. But because I'd taken Advanced Placement English in high school and scored well, I was able to skip the introductory course and head directly into a seminar on Shakespeare. My roommate, however, did have to struggle through *Paradise Lost*, which was harder for a nice Jewish girl from a public high school in a Boston suburb than it might have been for a lapsed Catholic brought up in a Brooklyn diocese. After all, Iris had to learn this stuff about Christianity because it was expected that every student already knew it. The assumption seemed to be that any student at Dartmouth would have been prepared—between their own family's religious background and all that compulsory chapel they had to attend at their schools—to embark on Milton's journey from the "felix culpa" in Eden to the redemption of humanity by the coming of Jesus Christ.

"I thought 'felix culpa' meant 'the cat is to blame,'" Iris complained.

She bought the notes to *Paradise Lost* as if she was buying pornography. One day, Iris came back to the room and summed up the class as follows: "What we learn from *Paradise Lost* is that if one woman can lead a man into sin in Eden, imagine what a whole bunch of them are doing to Hanover." That was the idea: that women push men into paradise, transforming them—against their will, yet—by appealing to their appetites. A woman is a carbon copy of a man; she is slightly more faded and missing some essential piece of humanity. "He for God, and she for God in him," Milton declared. She was human but once removed. She was human in translation. Iris was pissed.

But I loved my freshman seminar, even though, in retrospect, it may have led to my determination to teach at a public university. My professor, a twenty-eight-year-old man of much charm and wit, passed back our first papers and flicked out the remark: "Luckily it's early enough in the term for most of you to find places in state colleges." He meant it to be funny. It sounded, then and now, hollow and ruthless.

I also heard, for the first time that year, an upper-division student saying as a half-joke, "It is not enough to succeed; others must fail." I recalled the bonfire and the idea that it was only fun if the process was adversarial.

Looking at the competition was bad for me. I could never look at the competition and keep my balance. I wasn't like the girl from our high school who memorized the SAT scores of most of the senior class. One look back and I was done for. Only with a blinkered vision of my own competence might I be able to stay the course.

But even those first few weeks were not all gruel and ashes. Yes, to an extent barbarism was formalized into the fraternity system, but there were a couple of guys I actually liked who just happened to be part of the system. There were great teachers, great dances, great roommates and friends, great evenings at the Bull's Eye, a dark-paneled, smoky bar. There was an infamous tea at the Hanover Inn in celebration of a friend's October birthday where, unladylike as ever, I spilled Earl Grey down my one good dress. I went to the ladies' room, took the dress off, and dried it with paper towels. I emerged, damp and stained, but sat back down, unwilling to give up little white-bread cucumber sandwiches that looked almost too cute to eat.

My appetites, it seemed, would see me through most embarrassing occasions.

Most of my pals, male and female alike, were also part of the dispossessed in some way. Too urban, too shy, too ethnic, too working class, too outrageous, too intellectual, too subversive to be accommodated by the mainstream, we formed our own Dartmouth.

We went in our Texan friend's Gremlin to the Four Aces diner, a ribbed-vinyl-seat sort of place where chipped-nail-polish waitresses kidded around, and where we ate French fries drowned in gravy. We went to the Riverside Grill, where short-order cooks yelled out pick-ups from the kitchen and the waitresses called us "Doll" or "Hon" when they came to the table to put down two slices of buttered white bread per customer. We sang "You Picked a Fine Time to Leave Me, Lucille" with everyone else when the song came out of the jukebox. These were decidedly town, not gown, joints. Here we were miles from a library. We walked endlessly around Occum Pond, slightly worried about the bats and the occasional stray dog, and talked about what we'd do in ten, twelve, fifteen years. We were relieved to realize that nobody had any idea except for one guy who wanted to be an actuary—and we spent a lot of time trying to talk him out of it once we found out what it was.

We argued with each other and lambasted the system even as we found comfort and support in this place we made for ourselves. But even when I was enjoying myself, I wanted to get through my early days at Dartmouth as quickly as possible.

There are lapidary moments. I remember a compassionate and brilliant teacher (who has since left the profession) telling me not to wish my life away. "These days, one by one, will be important to you in ways you can't possibly imagine. They are the beginnings of things to come. Don't underestimate them." I wrote down those words. Now I make my undergraduate students write them in their own notebooks. This teacher also had a poster on the back of the door to his office. It featured Miss Piggy from the Muppets dressed as an astronaut, and in huge letters blared "PIGS IN SPACE!" It was great. I would sometimes show up during office hours just to visit the *poster*.

If there's one lesson from my freshman year, that was it. Not that pigs can fly, but that big things begin when you're not expecting them, when you're not looking. It happens in history and it happens in life. One morning there was moveable type. One morning there was chloroform for operations. One morning there were spur tracks set up for runaway trains. And one morning you wake up and you're in love, or you're breaking up with your boyfriend from home, or you've aced your exam. One morning you wake up and nothing is ever the same again.

We were splitting up and forming new lives, even though we didn't know it. We were no more conscious of the process than cells dividing in a petri dish.

Risking Dartmouth was, after all, worth the fear and anxiety. Risking loneliness, I found lasting companionship. Risking rejection, I found an odd sense of acceptance. Risking failure, I discovered native ability and laboriously honed it into skill. Risking unhappiness, I found at least measured and memorable joy. Risks are worth it.

After all, you can always take the next bus home.

14. *Conversations*

Advice from Tiger, a sophomore, on signing up for classes:

"Get there early. You stand in line and go through this whole bizarre ritual. It's like doing the goddamn stations of the cross."

My brother Hugo and the Skylark.

 15.

Classes begin, and once again Good Girl Gina sits up front. The American lit. professor appears to be a bulky, middle-aged, heavy-set, tweedy, standard-issue type. Wire-rim glasses perched on a long patrician nose, sparse white hair, broad chest, and deep voice all add to the sense that he's straight out of central casting. Gina feels this is what college is all about.

Then the professor opens his mouth.

He announces at the start, "My name is MANN, I am teaching a book about a sperm whale named Moby Dick. Anybody who has a *problem* with that can leave right now. I have been teaching here for thirty years and I am not about to change my ways because there might *suddenly* be in my classroom a *delicate flower* whose *feminine sensibilities* I might *offend.*" He pauses, and walks over to a large, beefy guy in the first row and puts his hand on the young man's shoulder. "And I'm not referring only to Pemberton here, either, although he is known to be *sensitive.*"

Applause breaks out, whoops and hollers. Pemberton is clearly delighted by the attention and raises his fist in triumph. The professor moves around the large room, stopping by students who sit at the ends of their rows. His wet, rheumy eyes fix on his listener; he has a habit of leaning forward so that his breath, full of Johnny Walker Black, coffee, and pipe, is warm on the face. His physical presence is as overbearing as his ideology and as difficult to overlook.

Gina buries herself as far as possible into her seat. How can you be a Good Girl in a place that doesn't want any kind of girl whatsoever?

She sits with some new people at lunch. The girl is named Galetea but goes by the nickname "Snooks." The boys are named Forest, Artemus, and Cathcart but are called "Nutman," "Rocks," and "Crabgrass" by their friends.

Iris comes back from having had a class with—astonishingly enough—a female professor.

"She says that gender is important in how we interpret the world," Iris explains.

"You mean sex? Even my aunts know that. What's this class going to teach you that you couldn't learn at Coney Island?"

"Not sex, gender. They're different."

"I don't want to be treated differently because I'm a girl. I just want to be a Dartmouth student."

"But that isn't possible here—we're always going to be seen first as women because being female at this college is like being a pioneer in a covered wagon."

Gina worries that she might be nuts because, even in this class with Mann, all she wants is just to fit in. She thinks it will be easier to fit in than stand out.

She is wrong.

16. *Conversations*

Tiger often makes the argument that women on campus should not be flattered by being treated differently from male students, even when it might appear to work in their favor.

"This is not a gift horse," advises Tiger, "this is war. You should always look in its mouth."

17.

During philosophy class, I am listening to the professor—a younger man, dressed in his regulation tweed jacket—tell the story of a Chinese philosopher who dreamed he was a butterfly and then couldn't decide whether he might not be a butterfly dreaming he was a Chinese philosopher. An incredibly good-looking guy leans over and scribbles across the margin of my brand-new spiral notebook, "You think there's a butterfly somewhere dreaming he's a moron philosophy professor?"

I decide this boy could write across my curriculum *anytime*. Tall, dark eyes, haughty face, theatrical backsweep of dark hair, he looked like a junior, maybe even a senior. Impressed but skeptical, I wonder "Why is he in an introductory class?" I had an excuse: it was my first week of college. But why was he there when he looked older?

And why did he choose me? There were all these beautiful blonde girls with perfect skin and long tanned legs that appeared straight from their middle, no hips or thighs, so that from the waist down they looked like tweezers. Would he and I end up dating? Would we get married and have impossibly beautiful children and build a house with our own hands and tell our sophisticated and delightful close friends the story about how we met in this hothouse of a philosophy class? Would this mean I would not have to worry about taking the GREs in four years? If I could talk this guy into marrying me, maybe I could get out of applying to law school.

It occurs to me that maybe he's thinking of a much briefer attachment, one lasting about fifteen minutes.

Would I ever stop thinking about guys and start thinking about life?

I thought about Michelle Yankovitch who, at our high school graduation, proudly displayed the wedding gown she wore under her borrowed robes. The Yankovitchs had declared their daughter could get married any time after she got her high school diploma.

Michelle was the literal type.

Maybe she had a point, I think as I sit there desperately trying to pay attention. Would it have been easier to get married and stay in the neighborhood? I probably could have talked some poor soul into it.

Maybe Michelle *did* look like she just escaped from a group home, but now she was *settled*. She was lucky. She didn't have homework, even if she did have housework. There were no deadlines for her. No exams. She could sleep in every morning with her babies and watch reruns of *I Love Lucy*. All anybody would ever expect was that she keep the kids and the apartment clean; if she so much as put on *lipstick* it would count as a big night. If she balanced the checkbook every month they'd throw a *parade*. She had a purpose in life. She could get fat and breathe easily.

"A table is merely the currency we exchange, the concept we invent, to represent the irrepresentable," the professor intones. I write it down although I have no clue what he means.

"Michelle," I think while trying to listen to the definition of reality offered by the philosophy professor, "Do you ever wish you were me?" And all I, College Girl, could wonder was "Should that be 'Michelle, do you wish you were I'?"

I can't shake the ghost of Michelle: three hundred miles away and she still bothered me. "Michelle is probably decorating a cute little apartment and has some easy job somewhere, plus she's having sex every night with that nice boy Harold," I could hear my Aunt Josie saying.

Michelle never could have made it into this fancy school, not to mention that this handsome boy sitting next to me would never have written her a note, even for the hell of it, so why was I secretly envying her? Because all the big questions in her life looked like they were already answered? Because when she thought about a table, she only had to think about a matching dinette set? Michelle probably had new chairs, *real* chairs, not just representations of chairs.

Me, I am perched uneasily on a walnut seat that has been worn smooth by several centuries of male behinds.

If, as a family friend who sells used cars once explained to me, "there's an ass for every seat," which chair is mine supposed to be in?

And where is the handsome guy going to sit in the next class?

18. *Conversations*

After a few beers, one giggling girl admits to another:

"I used to cheat in high school by writing answers on Chiclets and then eating them but I'm too scared to try that here. Very few people chew gum."

19.

I figured the male/female ratio worked in my favor. There were five men for every woman on campus. I thought I had it made.

Since the administration thought it best to get the alumni accustomed to the idea of coeducation by sneaking us in a few at a time, I thought I had terrific odds in my favor socially. How could I lose? I was no Miss Budweiser, true, but I thought even a gargoyle would have no problem getting a date every Saturday night.

Right away, however, I noticed an unnerving pattern. I'd meet a cute guy at a party and talk for a while. We would then be interrupted by some buddy of his who would drag him off to another room to watch a friend of theirs "power-boot" (the local vernacular for "projectile vomiting") and I realized that the social situation was not what I had expected.

Then somebody explained to me that on this campus "they think you're a 'faggot' if you like women more than beer." This statement indicated by its very vocabulary the advanced nature of the sentiment behind it. If a guy said he wanted to spend the weekend with his girlfriend, for example, he'd be taunted by his pals who would yell in beery bass voices, "Whatsa matter with you, Skip? We're gonna get plowed, absolutely blind this weekend, then we're *all* gonna power-boot. And you wanna see that broad again? Whaddayou, a fag or something?"

It turned out that the male-female ratio did not prove to be the marvelous bonus I had anticipated. But still I figured that the school was good enough to justify spending the next few years getting down to studying and forgoing a wild social life. I thought it would all work out, that at least I would be accepted in my classes as a good student and get through the next couple of years without too much worry or trouble. I told myself that I could live with that, especially since I was dating a guy from a different school anyway.

But the real shock came in the classroom where I was often one of two or three women in the group. Professor Mann, for example, always prefaced his question to me or any other girl in the class by asking, "Miss so-and-so, *as a woman*, what is your reading of this text?" I was profoundly embarrassed to be asked my opinion as a woman, since it seemed somehow less authoritative than being asked my opinion as a student or as a "general" reader. At first, I jokingly replied that I would be happy to answer "as a person," but that it was hard for me to answer *as a woman*. When the professor didn't so much as smile, I knew that tactic wouldn't work. Every time I raised my hand to answer a question, I was asked my opinion *as a woman*. It frustrated and angered me, because I wanted to be treated as an individual and not as a representative of a group.

It took months to understand that in the eyes of this teacher, I'd always be a "Miss" rather than just an ordinary student. When I realized that there was no alternative, I figured I'd go with it, exaggerate the situation enough so that I could at least enjoy myself. So I started prefacing every answer with the phrase, "As I woman, I think Shakespeare means . . .," "As a woman, it strikes me that Tennyson's point is . . ." But then I figured, why stop at this? I started to say "As a woman, I think the weather's rather cold for June." "As a woman, I think I'll have the meatloaf for dinner." It started out as a joke, but as it caught on (a number of my friends started to use the same strategy to make the professors and guys in general hear how their remarks sounded), we started to examine further. Maybe we really were always speaking as a woman. Maybe there was no such thing as speaking as "just" a person. Maybe we always spoke as women whenever we spoke. Maybe this joke wasn't such a joke.

So that even as I stopped saying "As I woman, I believe such-and-such," I started thinking it. It occurred to me that nothing was neuter or neutral. I saw that my responses were determined in part by the fact of my gender—as well as by other factors such as my class and ethnicity. I didn't read novels about war in the same way a man would, for example, since I hadn't been brought up to consider going to war as a soldier as a possible future for myself. I hadn't played war games as a kid, I didn't find the idea of war engaging. It did not have "universal appeal" since it didn't appeal to me, a narcissistic but nevertheless compelling argument.

In the same way that the male students complained that Jane Austen was obviously a second-rate writer because all she was interested in was marriage (Mark Twain once said that it was "a pity they let her die a natural death"), so I decided to assert that Hemingway's concern for bullfighting was no concern for an intelligent woman. Of what interest is bullfighting to the contemporary female reader? Hemingway was therefore second-rate, by their definition, since his subject matter had limited appeal and seemed gender-specific. I learned to answer "Of course" when asked whether I responded to things as a female. I learned to accept that and even enjoyed discovering the ways in which my viewpoint differed from the perspective offered by my male peers.

But even understanding that the world identified me first as a woman and only secondly as anything else didn't stop me from being horrified the first time somebody called me a "feminist." I thought being a feminist meant I couldn't wear lipstick or crave men with small behinds. I thought that "feminist" meant I couldn't send "Peanuts" cards to guys who I was afraid wouldn't call back, or buy stockings with seams. I thought "feminist" meant no more steamy flirtations or prolonged shopping trips. I thought it meant braided hair and short nails, maybe mandatory tofu. I certainly associated feminism with humorless, earnest women. That was because I was accepting the male version of things, which was like believing the mouse's version of the cat: all the mouse can see is its claws.

I was warned about so-called feminists. I was told by boyfriends, relatives, professors, and other reputable sources that such women were ambitious, sharp-tongued, a little too smart for their own good. They told me that only women who couldn't get laid got political. They told me that independence and ambition were unattractive in a woman. They also suggested that being funny was sexually unappealing.

None of this, of course, turned out to be true.

Luckily, I heard a female graduate student from the geology department repeat a wonderful line from writer Robin Morgan, "*We are the women that men have warned us about.*" It was as if the little lightbulb that appeared over Bugs Bunny's head when he got an idea suddenly appeared over mine. It unnerved me to realize I had spent years criticizing qualities that I possessed. I was certainly ambitious, ready to speak, and eager to defend my position on a subject. I liked being a woman, was proud of my femininity, and believed myself to be equal to any task set before me.

So, when I really thought about it, I was already a feminist no matter what I chose to call myself. When I looked around, I saw a lot of smart, funny women who also fit the bill. We were all feminists, whether or not we'd admitted it aloud before. It was sort of like admitting we were secretly Bad Girls, and for me the admission held the same sort of delightful relief. Oh, is *that* what I am? Is this what the word means, is this what the name names? Is this what a feminist is? Excellent.

Feminists like to dance, flirt, and wear high-heels, often doing all three at the same time. Feminists can like men—and enjoy the process of liking individual men for their own worth instead of valuing all men simply because they're male. Feminists enjoy and value the company of other women. Feminists don't wish they were men; they celebrate their sex—and, as Iris's professor would say, they celebrate their *gender* as well.

And women have a particular way of using humor to survive. We certainly did at Dartmouth.

Whether you choose to call it feminist humor, or feminine humor, or "just" humor, if you're a woman then you're making a woman's joke, laughing a woman's laugh. In the same way that we can't help but speak as women, we can't help but be funny as women. We're inevitably informed by our gender. You're taking on a new perspective, offering your statement or question when the system would encourage you to be silent. When you make a joke, when you laugh with your mouth open, or when you refuse to laugh at something you don't find funny even though you know you "should" laugh, then you're making a radical gesture. You're ignoring the script that tells you when to speak (almost never) and when to laugh (when someone else tells you to).

I'd say that any time a woman breaks through a barrier set by society, she's making a feminist gesture of a sort. And every time a woman laughs out loud—any time a woman makes a noise that isn't a whimper or a cooing sound—she's breaking down a barrier.

I was convinced no one would ever get it—that I'd spend all my days living inside my own head. I dragged myself to Thayer Hall for lunch one ugly day, banging my tray down onto the counter and loading it with diet soda and cheesecake. I saw a girl from my French class whose name I didn't know. I decided it would be too weird not to acknowledge her.

"I know we're in a class together," I said. "Which is it?"
"Upwardly mobile," she said, biting into a hard roll.

I felt right at home. And it felt good.

And suddenly I loved everybody from the American lit. class, and the handsome nameless boy from philosophy, and my roommate Iris, and the defiant insider Tiger, and the girls I studied with at the library, and I loved Professor Scaldini from French and even my Shakespeare teacher. It was a nameless emotion—it went off in too many directions, like a firecracker exploding into color against a

July night's sky. I could only sit with my feelings as they skyrock-
eted, illuminating places in my life that I had feared might be dark
for four years.

🐜 20. *Conversations*

Boy, clearly interested, to a girl, equally intrigued:

"What perfume are you wearing?"
"Do you like it? It's patchouli oil."
"It smells like dirt."
"Like dirt?"
"Not like *filth,* just like dirt."
"That's just great. 'Not like filth' is terrific. Were you raised by
wolves? Didn't anybody ever teach you how to talk to girls?"

🐜 21. *Conversations*

At a party at the River Cluster dorms, Iris and I hear a drunk guy
singing in a lyric, earnest voice, the following words to a popular
Moody Blues song:

"Whites in night satin, never reaching the end . . ."

Iris wonders, unkindly, whether "there's a silent 'k' in there?" Tiger
hisses, in a stage-whisper, "Should we ask him to start singing 'If I
Were a Hammer . . .'?" I giggle so hard that I need to leave the room.

But I never again hear "Nights in White Satin" without reversing
the words.

22.

We were sitting in Tiger's huge off-campus room, slumped over chairs and draped across beds as if we were the skins of endangered animals. Iris was sitting near the window and pretending to read, Liz was methodically tearing the cuticles off her fingers, Brenda had her eyes closed, Tiger was drinking her second mimosa even though it was just noon, and I was lying on my stomach across the delicate patchwork quilt on Tiger's bed like I was on a stretcher just waiting to be carried out feet first. We were all silent for once.

So when I muttered, "Aside from every other bizarre thing about this place, you've GOT to believe that a boy's college with the unofficial motto 'It May Be Small, But There Are Those Who Love It' suffers from a *inherent* lack of self-reflection," everybody turned to look at me.

"The real words are 'It May Be a Small College But There Are Those Who Love It," yawned Violet, who already wanted to be copyeditor at *The Daily Dartmouth.*

Taken from a speech made by one of the college's founding fathers who wanted to keep the institution a college and not make it into a university, the line was not a joke. It was, however, ubiquitous. It greeted every arriving student when you walked into the dining hall. It kept greeting you, mercilessly, because it was printed, stamped, woven, or embossed on everything: T-shirts, gym shorts, towels, dining hall trays, mugs, flags, notebooks, and nightshirts. The nightshirts were displayed in the college bookstore's window, cheerfully hanging below a sign blaring "Great Gifts for That Special Girl!" The sign suggested that the campus had not adjusted to the fact that women were now actual full-time, legitimate students at what had always been an all-male college. I didn't have a "special girl" in my life. Was I my *own* special girl, perhaps? Who could I buy one of these for? I didn't think getting nightshirts with "It May Be Small, But There Are Those Who Love It" printed across the bust line would be appropriate as a way to indicate to my short, round Brooklyn aunts that they were special.

But in Tiger's room, when I admitted out loud that the college's "Small and Those Who Love It" obsession was too weird for words, Tiger, Brenda, Liz, and Violet were all silent for half a second. Then we all started to laugh like banshees, wiping the mascara away from under our eyes (even Tiger, who never wore mascara, was doing this eye-wiping gesture), catching our breath, and talking all at once. "Can you believe we have to get our contraceptives fitted at a health-care center called 'Dick's House'?" "You think the bonfire has any phallic symbolism attached?" "How about the other night when I had to stop dancing with that guy because he had absolutely no sense of rhythm and to make up for it, he starts telling me a joke about King Kong getting a blow job. Like *that* was what I was hoping to hear all night?" "I feel like I'm breaking up a stag party every time I walk into a classroom." "You too?" *"Really?"*

We were well on our way to colonizing the place, even though we didn't know it.

🐾   23.

During those first days of classes, the place resembled a medieval city: there were too many people, too much noise, too much confusion, too many competing voices for a person to make sense of this routineless-routine. Not to mention the fact that in those mid-'70s days, buck shoes, tight white pants, and striped T-shirts were making a decided return. It was not, to put it mildly, a very pretty picture.

Densely and ostentatiously furnished, the financial aid office boasted photographs dating back to 1911. I thought of how those boys voted against accepting women into their institution and I wanted to stick out my tongue at their little faces and go "nyhh, nyhh." The administration buildings had mushroom-colored walls and some lobbies boasted furniture with all the shape and texture of marshmallows. I feared sitting down and getting absorbed into one of those chairs, never to be heard from again. I mean, I was *intimidated* by the furniture. This was not healthy.

24. *Conversations*

Lying together under a tree, having a picnic and an emotional moment, a boy tells a girl, who gently weeps:

"Please stop crying." He sounds like he really means it.

There is a pause before he explains, "Your tears are making my *armpit wet*."

25.

"My aunts taught me to dance," I said to the beautiful boy from my philosophy class while we were sweeping across the floor of a frat house. He was as different from everyone I'd ever met as I was from everyone he'd ever met. It occurred to me as he brushed his hand against the back of my neck that my grandparents would have been working in factories his grandparents owned, that my uncles would have been fixing his father's shoes, that my aunts would have been sewing his mother's dresses, and that, in only a slightly different world, I would have been the nameless waitress at a place he went for coffee. But the world had shifted, however slightly, on its axis and we were locked together in a moving embrace, presumably as equals.

When I looked up at him, I felt what I could only identify as my stomach contracting, like someone sketching a detailed picture on my belly like ice skates on a frozen pond. But what was happening that evening was the beginning of a thaw, of a new season having nothing to do with winter.

That was the night I found out that dancing lets you take a stranger and hold him in your arms, and that such holding is one of the best things about it. You move together, briefly and silently. I was so conscious of my body while I danced with the beautiful boy that my fingers still remember the feeling of the skin on the back of his hands, of the slight pressure of his leg brushing against mine, and the way I felt my mouth forming words for the sheer pleasure of making my lips move so near to his that he must have felt my warm breath on his throat.

I thought about where he must have grown up, in a quiet house tastefully decorated.

Most of my relatives lived in houses decorated in Sicilian Gothic, full of small rooms where you could always find a crucifix and a corkscrew. In these rooms you could always find people telling contradictory stories.

And you could *always* find music, Louis Prima or Dean Martin, with an aunt or two tapping her feet to the beat.

One thing all my female relatives could do was dance. Dancing with my mother, who loved to jitterbug, was always a great joy. My little fat aunts, too, could dance, gracefully, wildly stamping their improbably tiny feet and flinging one another around the room to juke box music off the cheap red radio. When I was little they swung me around like longshoremen unloading cargo. With one another they practiced the intricate moves, raising eyebrows and half-smiling when they got it perfectly right, when fingertips touched just as the music stopped. It didn't have a name, but it was the only dance they knew. And it was great.

When I was about thirteen, we went to a cousin's wedding. I wore a cheap dress in a deep green color: I looked like an avocado. I pleaded homework and cramps, but there I was, on the way to a hotel in Queens, backseat window rolled up against the breeze from the river, curls of hair, like snails, already damp against the back of my neck. Something was different in the slick, false ballroom. The cake was a cartoon, vaulted high as a cathedral.

The bride and groom walked in, black and white with her red bouquet like a blush in her arms. We all knew what they were thinking. Yet the priest had blessed them and what five minutes before was a slap-in-the-face sin was now a sacrament, sanctioned by God between the marital sheets. Anything could happen.

Old ladies in purple and black looked like eggplants, moving together around the perimeters of the room until the music started.

The music was magic. It was like Lourdes. Women who had hardly walked in years got up to dance. They laughed and smiled, doing dances as old as their whisperings, dancing done for harvests and fertility.

Something in me thumped in recognition, but when Aunt Grace pulled me in I pulled myself out. I wasn't ready. But I was ready to dance with the friends of my cousin, rough boys with black hair, boys from vocational schools, boys otherwise out of bounds. My skirts flung out, my legs showed, and for a minute fear raked nails across my arched back. But everybody was smiling. It was a wedding. I danced harder, as if something depended on it, until my father's hand, reaching through the music, pressed against my shoulder to say we had to go. Looking at my partner, he said, "The long drive back . . ." The boy nodded and I smiled like a chorus girl, thinking the green dress brought out my eyes and fitted me as closely as felt on a pool table. My cousin's husband, like a tycoon in his striped tie, kissed his wife as we were leaving. The wedding guests rapped spoons against their glasses in a fine silver shower of sound. My new shoes were like little boats of pain but I didn't mind; I could hear every note in the music like you hear your own name in a crowd. Who cared that the band wasn't good; who cares who calls your name so long as somebody shouts it?

The aunts who danced on Saturday evening went to church on Sundays and some went during the weekday, too, to cover their heads with lace and cry. Churches locally seemed filled with women in mantillas weeping and making excuses. The pews also held a few frowning men, making their own excuses, looking more defiant than unhappy when confronting their Maker with their own sinfulness. My talent, clearly, was for breathlessly overhearing things, not minding my own business, and storing away what I did not understand, in order, it seems, to invent interpretations that only coincidentally coincided with the truth.

So that while I did not know specifically for what sins my aunts cried in the brick churches, I figured that these sins must have happened in the past. Surely they were incapable of sinning at their advanced ages. Sinning was a youngster's game, something to look forward to for me, and something to look back on for them. My aunts led complex lives in a simple setting, and I, wrongly, thought I had their story straight before I was even starting my own. I thought their marriages, their loves, their passions, their furies, were diluted by their years and buried by their shapeless flowered dresses.

I separated myself from their circles, and found other rhythms strumming beneath my feet.

So in the arms of the philosophy-class boy, I was glad I wore perfume in my hair. I was glad that my hair was long and for the first time I was really glad that it was black and curly because everyone else's was straight and fair. He could ask, "What happened to the girl with the curly hair?" and it could be only me he was asking about. If he asked at all, that is. Who knew what he was thinking? Maybe he was thinking about the girl he came with, a small-faced woman who wore pearls and clean shoes, and who kept an eye out for him while I kept my eye on her.

I was thinking about this boy taking my hand and then pulling me toward him, his hands in my hair, his mouth against mine. I was thinking of nights when I was sixteen in the long backseats of cars with one-night-stand boys, never going below the waist dictated by morality and a need not to have to bother: who needed to be *that* busy on those July evenings? I was remembering hands on my breasts and kisses that went on for hours and the deep hunger for tongues and sweat and breaths that were as shallow and as far-reaching as a stone skipped across a pond. Every moment scratched on the tender surface of the stretched and transparent membrane fine as a cornea, arched, humming like a tuning fork, quivering like a divining rod, full as a bucket and heavy as water.

In my head I told him, "Dancing with you is a dressed rehearsal, an upright version of a deed with a downside. Threading my fingers with yours as if we are playing a child's game of church and steeple is for me at least only a prelude to the grown-up game. Your leg against mine even in a dance is no game; my hand spread open against your back and feeling the movements of your shoulder with my fingertips is no mechanical motion. Slipping muscle against bone as you maneuver me across a polished wooden floor to music is serious, serious business." I tried to signal this message to him like a lighthouse or a secret agent, tapping it out in the unspoken but universally understood code of desire.

I tried to make him understand the message through the hieroglyphs of the heart, but he didn't hear.

He heard how I sounded, my voice—not my arms—capturing his attention. "Say that again," he said, dimpling his perfectly smooth cheek, keeping me inside the gravitational pull of his charm. I smiled because I didn't dare not smile in front of a handsome man, but I was puzzled. Whatever else he was blind to, he wasn't blind to my slightly blank look.

"Say what again?" I ventured, no doubt fluttering a few eyelashes for good measure; if I was going to look like a fool then at least I could also look like a flirt and pretend it was intentional. He smiled. "Say 'My aunts taught me to dance.' You have a real New York accent."

I didn't think of myself as having an accent. I didn't think of myself as bearing the stamp of difference every time I opened my mouth. Words had always been my allies, things I could count on. But that evening, for the first time, I heard myself the way he must have heard me, with a voice like Brooklyn traffic, saying "aunts" as if I were talking about insects instead of relatives. I didn't even try pronouncing the word differently. In part, I knew too well that by mimicking his way of saying "Aahnts" not only would I make myself ridiculous, but I would at that moment be swapping a strong and real inner-voice for something that was merely correct.

Maybe he genuinely liked what he saw in me that night. Maybe now, years later, I'm judging him unfairly, but I don't think my accent would have continued to charm him for very long.

The boy and I danced together only that one evening. He probably went on to dance slowly—but not too closely, never too closely— with the girl who had the pearls and the proper New England accent.

As for me, I learned to rely, increasingly, on my aunts' advice: life's too short to hold onto a guy who believes there's only one way to pronounce a word, or one way to move to the music.

I have moved across other dance floors in my day, small flat wooden countries full of miraculous mobility, slipping and regaining my footing, sometimes with a man's arm around me as a prop or a guide, sometimes just part of a circle of strangers or friends.

My aunts and my mother taught me better than I realized.

I follow in the quick, smiling grace of their footsteps.

26. *Conversations*

I ask Tiger why she doesn't want to meet the girl her boyfriend dated the year before. "Aren't you at least curious to meet the woman he was involved with for an entire year?"

"Nope," she replies. "If his old girlfriend is beautiful, I'll feel insecure. If she's ugly, I'll feel indignant."

Tiger helps me understand that a person should not ask questions if a person does *not* want to hear the answers.

🐝 *27. Scribbled in my notebook, 1975*

In all these relationships, it's basically the same. I worry: about liking him more than he likes me. About being possessive, jealous. Or even about being stronger sometimes, or smarter sometimes or more social sometimes. Although I get out quite a bit, I am not one of those women who flounces through life with an ankle bracelet, feather boa, and alligator shoes. I admire those women: I long for their absolute belief, not only that they are center stage, but that there is an audience. I have felt lately as if I am playing to an empty house. I want to do something, but the somethings I end up doing at these moments are bad, silly, stupid things. I eat everything I see without distinguishing one food group from another. Or I cut my hair with manicure scissors and look like Miss Havisham, which is who I'm afraid I'll end up becoming no matter what. Or I break something: a vase, a cassette tape, a mirror, risking bad luck.

🐝 28.

Ordinarily young people of nubile age are supposed to be shy of one another, and while tending herds pass one another by many times without apparently seeing each other. Around Camata, if a boy . . . wishes to take notice of a girl, he picks up a handful of fine earth or dust and throws it at her. This is a first step of courtship . . . The next time they meet, the boy picks up some fine gravel, and the girl may do likewise. If they continue to be interested this goes on until finally they throw rocks at each other. Informants told me that there were two cases of deaths in Camata during the last four years from such a cause; one woman received a fractured skull and the other a broken back.

> —Passage copied from an unidentified anthropology textbook,
> spring 1976.

🦟 29. *Conversations*

In the women's bathroom.

First girl: "Why do they like the girls from other schools better than they like us?"

Second girl: "Because they can drive them home. We're always right here, all the time, and you need to drive us away, not just drive us home, to get rid of us. Think about it. You can't deposit us in a different town. You can't escape somebody you slept with over the weekend and still go about your regular day. You'll have to see her. If she was in your class, she'd still be in your class. Besides, the girls from other schools bring them cookies and brownies and stuff. They help them type. They'll even do their laundry."

Third girl: "Where do I get me one of those people? That sounds amazing. Who wouldn't want one? Maybe if we all chip in?"

Second girl: "That's why some guys pay for sex. It's not the screw they pay for. They pay so that they can leave right away once it's over. And besides, some guys have emotional radar detectors. They can tell when there's serious relationship involvement down the road and they either slow down or steer clear."

First girl: "Is that part of being an alpha male?"

Third girl: "I don't want an alpha male. I want a beta male with a decent body and good stamina. I want a nice guy who will bring me a blanket who also happens to have muscles and chest hair."

🐝 30. *From my journal, fall 1975:* *"Girls from Other Schools Arrive on Buses"*

Lyrics to a song written, communally, by a bunch of women during dinner at Thayer Hall. The good news is that I can't remember the tune.)

> They come in their buses,
> they come in their cars.
> They come with their paints
> and they come with their jars.
>
> We stand on the Green
> and we watch them debark.
> Many look pretty
> and several look smart.
>
> When deep winter falls
> and we're stuck in the snow
> and it gets very lonely
> and there's nowhere to go,
>
> we'll look at the eyes
> of those next to us;
> we'll try to compete.
> And we'll curse the next bus.

🐝 31. *Conversations*

Late night, mostly drunk confession from a great guy, a kid from the Midwest, admitted in tones of shame and triumph mixed like gin and tonic:

"Big secret. Big, big, secret. I lied to get in here. On my application I said I had a heart transplant and that it was the biggest thing that ever happened to me. I explained that's why I wanted to be a doctor. But you want to hear something? I never had a heart transplant. My old man did though. But he died. Dropped dead, him and his new heart. Having him go through the whole transplant routine was like getting a fucking raise just before getting fired. It sucked. So I figured I might as well make the whole process worthwhile. My dad was a con man his whole life. For once he would've been proud of me."

  32.

My first digital clock was the one I bought to take to school. The idea was that *now* time was really precious. Now it mattered what I was doing with my days and nights because they were being paid for—if I wasn't working, if I wasn't in class, if I wasn't studying, if I wasn't doing some necessary task—eating, laundry, cleaning up—then I was throwing my time away like tossing dollar bills out a car window or throwing jewelry into the gutter. But the digital clock did not really help me keep track of my days and nights. Instead, it recorded, with its flip-thwack sound, the moments of my ever-increasing sense of indebtedness.

I worried a lot about money. Being poor at an unashamedly mon-eyed institution almost trumped being a girl at a boy's school.

The journey from being the child of a working-class family to a student at an Ivy League institution made accidental comrades of those of us who traveled the same but unfamiliar path. I don't expect or require plaintive violin music to accompany me here; I'm not Lillian Gish on an ice floe searching for retrospective rescue. I was never hungry. I was certainly never thirsty—it's tough to be thirsty at Dartmouth. I was often cold but that had at least as much to do with vanity and a bizarre sense of style (most specifically, a profound refusal to bring a garment stuffed with down anywhere near my person) as it did with anything remotely approaching poverty. Real poverty—the kind much of the world lives in, the kind much of rural New England and urban New York lives in, for example—I was fortunate enough to escape.

Even so.

In my senior year—more or less in secret—I applied to three schools: Queens College (near home), McGill University (in deference to my mother's heritage), and Dartmouth because the guy I was dating at another Ivy League school thought I should spend four years in Hanover making trouble. Not that he'd ever have gone to Dartmouth himself, mind you, but he had friends in Hanover who talked about the new female students. In retrospect I think he was looking at my college application process the way a kid might look at a makeshift chemistry experiment: let's see what happens if we add *this* to the mixture. The phrase is usually uttered from a reasonably safe distance so that if there's an explosion, mess, or any flying glass, no one will be hurt. When he heard that I filled out my application in peacock blue ink from a plastic cartridge pen, clueless about the fact that I should have been using a typewriter, he almost passed out.

Not that we owned a typewriter. That was my reward for being accepted into Dartmouth. My father bought me a huge and preposterous machine two weeks before college started, a typewriter the size of a Harley Davidson. I loved it. It was about as convenient as lugging a side of beef around with me at all times, but somehow it made me feel as if I were really a *bona fide* college student. When I got nervous, to reassure me my old man would ask, simply, "What's the worse that can happen?" Even when the worst didn't happen, I was still genuinely terrified.

On a number of other levels, however—and maybe you have to remember what it was like to be eighteen and out of your league to really get this—it was genuinely terrifying. Nice people asked me where my brother went to college and where my father worked. When I told them, they were slightly baffled by my answers and looked at each other dubiously to see if I were pulling their collective leg. Nice people asked me where I skied—I had never skied. Let's face it: I rarely went outdoors.

Even nicer people asked me if I wanted to go to local restaurants but I always worried that the money I made at my work-study jobs was not going to be enough to get me through to the end of the term and I didn't want to be a parasite. I sold my books back when I really wanted to keep them. I worried about being broke, about asking my father for cash, about the enormous number of loans I was taking out, and about small debts to friends. In the middle of some anxious nights, I wondered how I became a foster-child, however grateful, of this affluent institution.

My father and brother would drive up from Brooklyn once a term to visit me. Other folks' families came up and stayed for parent's weekend or homecoming but my dad and brother would drive back late the same night because it would never have occurred to any of us that they spend money on a room and stay for longer. They no more would have stayed at the Hanover Inn than I would have gone kayaking. In our family, we just didn't do that stuff. My brother would study the leggy, graceful girls, sleek as thoroughbreds, and comment on the disparity between them and my friends back home. I'd laugh along, chiding him, but I knew what he meant because the burnished, blue-eyed boys walking around campus looked pretty different from what I'd experienced back home, too.

What remained totally out of my reach was the polished look that comes from being a kid from a family with a solid financial and social foundation. We're not just talking good genes here, we're talk-

*My father, on the far left,
looking down, age 5, circa 1928.
With his brothers and sisters.
Brooklyn, New York.*

ing about something more complex, often referred to as breeding, a combination of inherited gifts and nurtured talents.

("All this good breeding is *bound* to rub off on you," a snotty sorority girl once quipped. "Not if I don't touch anything" I replied.)

As hard as it is to define, it is nevertheless essential to understand: fancy people—not necessarily the irrefutably rich, mind you, but the socially and culturally privileged—have a distinct way of handling the world, as if they are simply overseeing what belongs to them. I didn't have this and I couldn't fake it.

I also couldn't name it, couldn't get my mind wrapped around the concept until, in an independent study on the modern novel, I fell into a passage from John O'Hara's *Butterfield 8:*

all her life Emily had been looking at nice things, nice houses, cars, pictures, grounds, clothes, people. Things that were easy to look at, and people that were easy to look at; with healthy complexions and good teeth, people who had had pasteurized milk to drink and proper food all their lives from the time they were infants; people who lived in houses that were kept clean, and painted when paint was needed, who took care of their cars and their furniture and their bodies, and by doing so their minds were taken care of; and they got the look that Emily and girls—women—like her had.

I didn't have "the look," and so literally *couldn't* look at things from the same perspective. I had good grades and the stuff it took to get good grades. I had a bravado that often got mistaken for strength and a big mouth that was sometimes interpreted as self-confidence. And while I substituted swagger for poise and unashamedly used my sense of humor as a way to camouflage my almost perpetual discomfort, I couldn't fool myself or anyone else into thinking that Dartmouth was the kind of place that would have welcomed me.

Yet being at Dartmouth helped me recognize the contradictions in my own attitudes toward the traditional roles played out in my family; it also forced me to face—and even challenge—my own ambivalence about the larger implications of success. In retrospect, I think I both exploited and evaded the confines of the role of working-class-kid on campus. True, I saw social and economic spikes everywhere and rushed to impale myself on them, but I also, in time, came to accept that the education and experience were mine for good—not just things that had been lent to me, like somebody's earrings or their car, to be returned undamaged and unsoiled at a later date. A good education can be subversive, even when it apparently endorses conventional moral and cultural doctrines. I suspect, therefore, that only a very good education could have prepared me to be a troublemaker. I came to Hanover fearing trouble. I left looking for it.

EXPENSES AND RESOURCES WORKSHEET

Name _Regina R. Barreca_____ '79 Date _May 16, 1975_ By _JHD_

To help you in planning the management of your finances at Dartmouth College, we are providing you with this worksheet showing your expenses and resources as we have figured them for the fall, winter and spring terms of 1975-76. Please keep this sheet for future reference.

	Fall	Winter	Spring	Total
Your 1975 - 76 College Expenses				
Tuition	$1300	$1300	$1300	$3900
Room Rent Allowance	240	240	240	720
Meals	400	350	355	1105
Travel Allowance	25	25	25	75
All Other Expenses	280	210	210	700
TOTAL EXPENSES	2245	2125	2130	6500
Your 1975 -76 Resources				
From Your Parents or Guardian	135	150	140	425
From Your Off-Campus Earnings	200	200	200	600
From Your Past Savings	100	-	-	100
Basic Educational Opportunity Grant	108	109	109	326
Dartmouth Scholarship Grant	1300	1300	1275	3875
Long-Term Loan NDSL	400	125	175	700
Employment at Dining Hall	-	240	235	475
TOTAL RESOURCES	2245	2125	2130	6500

Please read again the leaflet enclosed with your award letter which was entitled "Dartmouth's Financial Aid Program," while you have this budget before you. If you have any questions regarding your finances for your freshman year, please don't hesitate to contact us.

We look forward to meeting you in the fall.

OFFICE OF FINANCIAL AID

Harland W. Hoisington Jr., Director
William C. Quimby, Associate Director
Jay C. Whitehair Jr., Assistant Director
Elizabeth M. Carr, Assistant Director
Judith H. Donner, Assistant to the Director

Dartmouth College Expenses and Resources Worksheet.

33.

"Never use your real name," my sly Uncle Bill used to say. I played with my name as if it were a toy. I cut it into pieces to look for a nickname. I spelled it different ways to see if could become more romantic, sleeker, or less ethnic. The name I tried to use as a grown-up is a name no one ever called me at home. It has taken me years to accept "Gina" as my real name. It is the name on my birth certificate, after all. The name looks round and easy. But in high school I wanted to be edgy and complex. Daily, I answered to the wrong name, wrote my essays in an alias, and told people how to spell my wrong name correctly. Nobody at home called me "Regina." That was for public consumption. That was me trying to sound like maybe I was secretly British. Like I could pass.

34. *Conversations*

"Two months ago all I thought about was how I wanted to make my relationship with my high school boyfriend work. But I guess relationships aren't like cars. You can't fix them according to an owner's manual. We had to break up. Yes, we did. Yes, I'll tell you why—you really want to know? He made love like he was *trying to park a car.* I could practically hear him tell himself 'a little to the left now, come on back, okay, okay, a little more to the left, straighten out . . .' And his attempts at foreplay? All the *subtlety* of somebody dialing a *rotary phone.*"

✿ 35. *From my journal, 1975*

Why am I always expecting to be taught a lesson? Why do I feel as if I will be punished into humility and gratitude even though I am busy filling my days with being humble and grateful? Why do I think I'm not worth anything and that I deserve even less than nothing?

Whose praise and forgiveness am I searching for? What voice do I need to hear? What voice can offer me redemption? Is it too easy to say that I'm scanning the airwaves for my mother's particular speech? Yes, I do realize that there is no phrase from her that reassures, only ones that threaten. I don't remember any lines and I'm good at remembering lines. Christ yes, I remember things she said, but none that help me. "It's not your father's second wife who will do for you what a mother does" does not help me; "Women shouldn't wear pants" doesn't help me; "Women who have children should stay home and take care of them" doesn't help me; stories of my father's impotence, his flirtations, his affairs, don't help me. As far as I can tell, declaring that I would end up pregnant, maybe married, certainly unemployed and probably unhappy didn't help me—I don't think those stories scared me into success. I think they just scared me. I think I'm still scared of them. I think I'm still scared of her.

I remember thinking she wouldn't come home from shopping, or going for a walk, and I was afraid that something bad would happen to her. What if she died while sleeping in my bed? She would, after all, come into my room and lie next to me if her restless insomnia disturbed my father. I remember very early on thinking that if I breathed at a different time from her I wouldn't die when she died. I can picture the scene sitting next to her at the movies. I remember laughter, it's true, but there were many more tears than laughs, and that's the real reality, not the nice stories my brother and I tell each other. The cute stories we tell about our mother are funny only in retrospect. She'd get lost driving in the same spot on the same highway every time we drove home from the beach. She'd be upset, but it became a family joke. Every time she went to the doctor it was a drama because she always thought every visit was the beginning of her death. At a certain point it was but Jesus help me if there was nothing in her life that became her like the leaving of it.

And me? I'm worse. Here am I, smarty pants, all stupidly nervous and calling attention to myself in the same neurotic way, resorting somehow to these old feminine tricks when I don't need to, when I can do better than this. The gravitational pull of fear is strong, and that pull, coupled with the magnetic center of habit, is pretty tough stuff to shake off. Maybe at some point it was useful, but it isn't useful any longer. Or maybe it's simply too good an excuse, one I can't resist but should resist, like Iris who can't keep candy in the room without eating it.

The temptation for me now is to vacate myself, to drown in oblivion. Not that I want to die exactly, but wouldn't it be easy to drink and take pills to make me sleep through this—this exam, this week, this semester? I could be peaceful; I could be quiet. Sleep. And maybe the seven dwarves would build me a glass coffin and a prince will ride up on a white horse.

Speaking of glass, last night I broke the frame to my high school diploma, the frame I bought only a couple of months ago, the one that I looked and looked at it as if it were something special. I was angry— the kind of angry I used to be a lot more of, and I wanted to blame somebody but I was all by myself. I was surrounded in this room by my anger and some broken glass. There was a dream around dawn where my mother warned me, "You're not allowed to be angry at those people who mean you no harm." Easy for her to say, shrouded, and dead safe, in my sleep.

🐜 36.

I was obsessively careful about birth control. Yet almost every month I worried about getting pregnant. I didn't understand why so many other girls appeared to be way beyond the petty treacheries of their monthly periods. The secrets of life were laid bare to them early. They knew how to drink without getting drunk and they knew how to screw without getting pregnant. I never got over telling my first real boyfriend that I was a day late and seeing the doors in his eyes slam against me. The endless nervous waiting for pain to pull into my belly like a train, signaling my freedom. Promises that I'll be good from now on, never exactly defining what "good" means so that I don't have to pay up. Oh please, Oh please. When my period finally came—as it always did—I would feel an immediate sense of elation, like winning at the slots, like shoplifting, like finding money on the street. Getting away with something. Again.

🐜 37. *From my journal, 1975*

One voice tells me I'm not the worst student in the world and other voices tell me to get out before I waste any more time. I don't know which voice is right. My inner life is misshapen. If I move with confidence, it is only because I have compensated for the grotesque nature of my true self. Thinking of myself as "good" academically is like thinking of myself as thin: hard to get used to even when some kind of objective criteria—a bathroom scale or a decent GPA—are recording a successful score.

Dartmouth College   HANOVER · NEW HAMPSHIRE · 03755

Office of the Dean of Freshmen · TEL. (603) 646-2681

Parents Letter #3

December 23, 1975

Dear Parents of '79:

Holiday Greetings to all of you and yours from all of us in the Freshman Office. I hope this message will reach you in time to say "Happy New Year."

Here in Hanover the campus is resting, recuperating. The town is in a vacation mood. Hopkins Center this week has staged a play, The Emperor's New Clothes, a carol sing, and a story hour. The Hanover fire engines are parading through the town, sirens howling, and each machine loaded with children riding to meet St. Nick, patron saint of the firehouse. I hope your '79 has had an equally exciting week and that you have been able to share some of his or her holiday whirl.

GRADES   If your son or daughter pauses long enough to discuss with you such ancient history as Fall Term marks, you may need a bit of background information. The old monotony of secondary school A's and B's may have disappeared. Your student may have brought you some alphabetical variety. Dartmouth professors have got as far along in their letters as D; some have even learned to print an E. Should your '79 have happened across such an advanced instructor you'll need a gloss of grades. The white flimsy sheet adorned with green rectangles is reasonably clear especially if you look at the flip side for "Explanatory Remarks." Yet the cluster of criteria surrounding each letter is not included. Let me give you in abbreviated form the criteria for the extremes of A and E. Here is what they are supposed to signify:

    A: 1. Excellent mastery of course material
        2. High degree of originality, creativity or both
        3. Excellent performance in analysis, synthesis, and critical
           expression, oral or written
        4. Student works independently with unusual effectiveness

    (Such a paragon should be worth an A.)

    E: 1. Serious deficiency in mastery of course material
        2. Originality, creativity or both clearly lacking
        3. Seriously deficient performance in analysis, synthesis, and
           critical expression, oral or written
        4. Cannot work independently

    Grade point values: A, 4; A-, 3 2/3; B+, 3 1/3; B, 3; B-, 2 2/3;
        C+, 2 1/3; C, 2; C-, 1 2/3; D, 1; E, 0.

You will be able without further guidance to bridge the chasm between A and E. Warning: you'll have to make a fair leap from 1 2/3 down to 1 and a real jump from 1 to 0.

Dartmouth College Parents Letter #3.

38.

My French-Canadian mother didn't teach me any French. I'd learned to decipher the words she'd throw around when arguing with my Italian father (who, incidentally, didn't teach me any Italian) but these weren't exactly words you'd use in a classroom. If there was any discussion of "*la plume de ma tante,*" it concerned an impolite reference to where you might insert *la plume.* I did, however, take four years of high school French and found myself, at the start of my first semester at college, placed into a class designed for students of moderate ability who had studied the language for several years.

It was a great class. The teacher was absolutely brilliant—funny, savvy, smart, and secure—and I felt lucky. I felt so lucky, in fact, that I began to understand how much French I *actually knew.* Within the first couple of weeks, I started to race ahead of some of my fellow students. The professor asked me to meet him for a conference whereupon he suggested, in all good faith and enthusiasm, that I'd be better off in a more advanced class. He thought I'd be more at home with more fluent students.

I took his advice. Why not? I was enormously flattered and wanted to rise to the occasion. As if I were leaving to go to Paris itself, I bid adieu to my companions in the lower ranks and headed off into more demanding, tempting, and unfamiliar territory.

I'm not saying it wasn't good advice overall; a gang of us in that advanced class got to know each other very well and have remained friends to this day. But I was way over my head in terms of the work; I could make myself understood when I spoke, but apparently this small talent deserted me completely when I tried to write. My essays came back full of green ink (the nice man avoided red, but the green was just as damning). I went to the language center tutors for advice. Tiger, whose great virtue was *not* patience but whose great talent was foreign languages, helped me straighten out the most basic of problems.

I got a C+ for the course—the lowest grade I ever received during my twenty or so years of education—and even that was a gift. (For all the current sanctimonious rigamarole about grade inflation, I'd like to point out that twenty-five years ago, at least at private colleges, almost nobody—and I mean nobody—got below what was called a "Gentleman's C" because the institutions were too afraid to alienate the families of students who might give big bucks to the joint.) I was relieved to see that I didn't have to repeat the course because I knew I wouldn't do much better the next time around. I simply had skipped over what should have been an essential part of my education but unless I was willing to takes months to rectify the situation, I had to accept my failure. Even if the grade didn't quite declare it to the outside world as "failure," everyone around me knew the truth. And I knew the truth.

I was disappointed in myself, but was grateful for the grade and grateful for the professor's confidence (even if it was misplaced). Over the years, I have grown grateful for the experience of knowing what it's like to sit in a class you love, work really hard, and still not be able to perform as well as you wish. This hard-won perspective has made me into a better teacher and a more understanding adult, as well as into a traveler who mostly avoids Francophone countries.

We discount the significance of failure. We see "failure" as "screwing up," or "messing around," or "not living up to potential."

People fail even when they do their best, when they mean well, when they work hard, when they are eager to please others and themselves. Coping with failure was a crucial thing to learn. The very notion of it (not its consequences, but its very *idea*) was the best thing I learned in that class and maybe in that year. *Vraiment.*

DARTMOUTH COLLEGE
REPORT OF GRADES

	CLASS	TERM
REGINA R BARRECA	79	75F
HINMAN BOX 0099		

SHORT TITLE	COURSE	GRADE	COURSE COUNT	GRADE UNITS	SELECTED REQUIREMENTS COMPLETED
					ENGLISH 5
FS-SHAKESPEARE	ENGL 007	B+	01	1	YES
					FRESHMAN SEM.
FREN CIVILZATON&CULT	FREN 003	C+	01	1	YES
EARTH HISTORY	GEOL 002	B	01	1	LANGUAGE
PHYSICAL EDUCATION	PE	CR	00	0	YES
					PHYS. ED.
CUMULATIVE TOTAL 04					NO

MAJOR	ADVISER	TERM. AVER.	CUMULATIVE AVERAGE ①	TOTAL INCMP.	DISTRIBUTIVE TOTALS ② HUMANITIES	SCIENCES	SOC. SCIENCES
	10672E	2.8	2.8888		1	1	

NRO, CT/NC USES AVAILABLE ③		NRO USES AVAILABLE ③		NUMBER OF C+ 'S OR BETTER ⑥		NUMBER OF D'S ④	
	8		3		3		

See Reverse Side for Explanatory Remarks

Dartmouth College Report of Grades for Regina R. Barreca, fall 1975.

🐜 39.

At the first suggestion of snow, I would fall down. On my ass. My inappropriate shoes and pink-sparkly fingernails would be useless in my attempts at getting myself upright. Witnessing such pitiful behavior, my friends took to circling me as we walked to dinner or to classes, creating a safety zone around my ridiculous self as if they were warriors circling against invading forces. We would be ignored by the more adroit students who, built with small heads and narrow shoulders—looking, basically, like thermometers—passed us effortlessly, upstanding.

40.

We were the members of Tau Iota Tau, one of Dartmouth's least official groups. Rather startlingly for a bunch of basically good girls raised in the cities and suburbs of 1960s and 1970s America, we made up a sorority in 1975 before any "real" sororities hit the campus—and we called it called Tau Iota Tau.

TIT.

Our motto was "They May Be Small, But There Are Those Who Love Them." Our colors were black and blue. You can imagine all the other jokes springing from this one-beat routine. We were uplifting. But the official Tau Iota Tau photograph is more compelling than I remembered it. One of my friends is wearing the varsity sweater she earned on the track team, but her waist-length dark and wavy hair betrays a less-than-Olympic attitude; one is wearing a feather boa, rhinestone earrings, and a gaudy T-shirt; another is holding a stuffed bison (that she claimed had been given to her in 1976, on the bisontennial); others could be mistaken for characters from *Cabaret, Annie Get Your Gun,* and *Threepenny Opera,* respectively.

As for me, I look like one of Dracula's wives, showing a vast expanse of bare throat rising up from a lacy, Gunny Sax dress I'd worn to my senior prom. I'm holding a bottle of champagne (which was more than just a prop), and I'm laughing. We don't look like Dartmouth students: even the girl wearing the varsity sweater looks like she stole it at gunpoint.

We were, as John Kemeny, the president during our tenure would have said, "Vomen of Dartmouth," but we didn't look like it. We didn't feel like it. Part of the reason for feeling as if Dartmouth wasn't completely available to me—or to many women I knew—

was the reflex response of "Honey-if-you-don't-like-it-here-why-the-hell-don't-you-just-leave?" if we dared to question business as usual. Why bother to imagine change if change seemed so unwelcome that the mere mention of it sent tribes of loyalists into seizures of frenzied "wah-who-wahs," chanting against the possibility of progress and potential?

The funniest thing happened, however, when we wrote a letter to the Dartmouth newspaper announcing our "sorority" after we heard that an official sorority was about to be launched. Whether or not it was true, we heard that you had to submit your parents' income tax form in order to be considered for that *real* band of sisters; it probably wasn't the case—I think there existed even back then laws prohibiting such initiation rituals, along with the slaying of goats— but it was probably pretty close. So our motley crew thought, what the hell, let's tell the world about our little gang. We signed our names and sent the letter in. A friend was the editor of the paper.

The paper printed it.

The response was immediate, and stranger than anything we could have imagined.

The young ladies who were starting the real sorority wrote a note to the paper—with a pink Flair pen, yet—saying in essence, "If these girls are so against our enterprise, why didn't they *use their real names?*"

We had. It was us, no disguise, no camoflauge. Our names were Barreca, Lager, Cohen, Rosen—with a handful of other names obviously unexpected for a Dartmouth by-line.

But the pink-Flair ladies thought *we made ourselves up.*

I was challenged time after time by guys in my classes, sometimes close friends, sometimes not, about why a woman wanted to attend

Moose sisters

To the Editor:

After reading Friday's article concerning the absence of sororities at Dartmouth, we felt it was our civic duty to finally declare ourselves to the Dartmouth community. There is a sorority on campus. It was formed by members of the Class of '79. Its name is Tau Iota Tau—the honorable sisters of the moose. We proudly wear our colors of black and blue beneath our conspicuous sorority pins.

In an exclusive interview, President Regina R. Barreca '79 was quoted as saying, "We've been trying to get a house somewhere in the Upper Valley, but the Moonies and other Aryan youth groups have top priority."

Not wanting to be just another "silly women's organization," like NOW, we propose concrete programs which will establish our identity as a unique social and intellectual group on campus. We have no wish to alienate our sisters from other schools, so we propose that Webster Hall be renovated to accommodate those poor, unfortunate "weekend visitors" who missed the bus early Sunday morning. Through such actions, we hope to increase the feeling of sisterhood (since that is what sorority means), and bring to life that age-old adage, "women need a sorority like a fish needs a bicycle."

We the sisters of TIT, invite all qualified women to apply for membership in this uplifting social group (cross our hearts!). And in closing, we wish to reaffirm our philosophy of "they may be small, but there are those who love them."

Regina R. Barreca '79, president
Nancy B. Lager '79, vice president
Janet ——
Carolyn ——
Esther ——
Natalie ——

The Tao Iota Tao, as printed in the Daily Dartmouth.

a "man's college." "If I'm here, then it's not a man's college anymore," I'd answer.

However, when my female contemporaries thought I was ficti-
tious, I figured I genuinely had it *made:* I could do *absolutely anything* I wanted because they didn't even think I was real.

It was almost too good to be true. And it gave me permission,
oddly enough, to be myself.

🐜 41. *Conversations*

A junior, discussing her most recent relationship:

"When Dad was posted in Belgium, I had a boyfriend who was at
University. He was a couple of years older, but he came from a good
family so my parents didn't mind. I traveled with him two sum-
mers ago, and I got to see most of Western Europe. Trouble is, I
didn't pay any attention to where I was because my entire life depended on whether or not Hans was in a good mood. I had no idea
whether we were in Vienna or Lyons or Manchester. The only thing
I had consciousness of was whether Hans was 'happy Hans,' 'frustrated and pouting Hans,' or 'silent, contemplative Hans.' I saw the
world through the many moods of Hans. Not a tour I would recommend, I must say."

🐜 42. *From my journal, 1976*

*Tap. Tap. Tap. Written words, ink words, do not have the clever preci-
sion of print and seem to present sentimentality and false modesty*

where there is none. One should be careful when writing longhand in ink, after dusk and before dinner, with no gently formal tapping of the keys acting like taps on the shoulder to keep one in line. Imagination both delights in and resents ink, seeing it as a medium for pictures, doodles, but rarely for correctly spelled and carefully sharpened ideas. Closed curtains over the windows and the heat turned on, clock ticking in a pedantic self-satisfaction, badly laid out desk.

Brown jars full of New Hampshire flowers, my matriculation certificate to prove I'm allowed to be here. Bulletins on the board facing me, so many papers and letters, each a guarantee of affection, vouchers of various kinds, books marked with pride in the margins offering questions and directions, but to whom? This year's view onto a garden which will, months from now, dutifully prepare roses. Bicycles in racks behind the garden. The days are getting shorter. But of course right now the curtains are drawn and this day, this garden, are already being drawn from memory.

 43.

I fell in love with nearly every male teacher I had from junior high onwards. It wasn't a healthy habit. My seventh-grade math instructor, Mr. Frisco, had a handlebar mustache, wore pop-art ties the size of dinner plates, and looked like an illustration from a Peter Max poster.

I wanted to be sure I learned his name right away, so I tried to figure out how to remember it. Not knowing there was a word for mnemonic devices, I nevertheless convinced myself that I could remember his name by thinking that it was a like a food shortening—Crisco—but with an "F." At his next class, I greeted him cheerfully, heart pounding beneath my black Danskin leotard. He asked me what I said. I replied, horrified, "I just said hi." "But what did you call me?" he asked. "I called you Mr. Fazola, isn't that right?" I realized, of course, what I had done the moment I opened my mouth: substituted Mazola for Crisco. But I could hardly explain that to him, blurting out "your name is like a cooking oil, but different," and so I had sabotaged myself in my longing for his attention and approval, which were the best substitutes I could find for his true love.

I pretty much shut up for the rest of the term, but I followed him around the school, sometimes secretly, sometimes boldly. Memorizing his schedule, I could just happen to walk by his classes as they were letting out and ask him questions. Never before had I been so inventive; never had I formulated theories both original and provocative about numbers. I got over being kept after school in fourth grade for not learning long division; I could not get over the sense that this handsome man and myself were bound by an inevitable attraction.

I bought him a book of short stories by Graham Greene for his birthday because my mother, with her inflated view of teachers, believed he would want only the very latest work by an important author. I now wonder whether he even knew who Graham Greene *was*, let alone why this tangled-haired kid was buying him books out of her allowance. He was the first teacher I fell for, but not the last.

I was a clever young girl, although I never excluded the low-cut dress for good measure, who had prepared a series of bright and well-formed answers to the threadbare questions handed to girls underage. I slept with my teachers forever. In eighth grade I was kept after English class to talk to Mr. Capp, and he was twenty-eight. Let me tell you, that seems old when you're half his age, when you're fourteen. He asked me what I liked to do; he was pulling down—no, not his trousers, this was 1971—but the afternoon shades, eclipsing all the natural light. I said I liked "making love" even though I was still a virgin.

I knew it would get a rise out of him. I wasn't sure what, exactly, would rise to meet me. What rose to the occasion was his gentlemanly self. I sat cross-legged on his desk in my gypsy outfit: thrift-shop skirt and hoop earrings. Willing if not eager, he remained a gentleman. He didn't touch me, and of course his look left far more of an impression than his fingertips ever would have. Or so I tell myself.

I fell in love with every professor I had in college, including the ones who looked like extras from the bar scene in *Star Wars*. There was no common denominator between them except for the fact that they stood up in front of classrooms where I sat, patient among rows of similarly enthralled and ripely under-age students. There were women on the faculty where I went to college, but not many, and besides, I wasn't particularly interested in taking their classes. I'd had plenty of women teachers all the way through school. Nice enough, I figured they offered nothing exotic. A guy in a tweed jacket, complete with wry smile and a knowing look: now *that* was exotic.

I didn't know that, at least up until 1985 or so, there was a fashion memo issued to all male would-be academics saying that they had to own at least one tweed jacket (preferably bought in England while they were doing a bit of research), one old, softly worn but brilliantly clean white shirt (washed by whose hands? I didn't allow myself to wonder), and one matching sardonic, wistful, perceptive hint of a smile to be brought out on infrequent but meaningful occasions, a smile that I looked for, longed for, and recorded in my notebook.

If only I'd known that the likes of me were cheaper by the dozen. Wiser men would have ducked when they saw us all getting off the train. We were every precocious, smart-mouthed, independent nineteen-year-old in tight jeans and a faded T-shirt. There was an army of us and we eagerly (not to say hungrily) invaded campuses around the country every fall. In the fall, we yipped and played like a litter of puppies, tossing each other around, pairing up and parting ways.

Things change, of course, after the fall.

After the fall, we started looking toward the grown-ups. We discovered favorite professors. We took first one, then more, of their classes. We brought cups of coffee to student conferences, and we met them late in the afternoon in the offices that took on new shadings toward sunset. They were, quite effortlessly and naturally, brilliant. They were concerned about the fact that not all of our peers were as insightful and wise above our years as we ourselves seemed to be. They were slightly sad about the way their own work was going, and there was a hint that this pall of melancholy also fell on other parts of their lives that they were too discreet to mention. They were disappointed in the lack of camaraderie among their colleagues, and puzzled that we, more than anyone, seemed to understand them.

We did independent studies. We found out more about their personal lives. We had a beer or two after the term was over to celebrate. There were longer silences, less talk, better papers, more research, higher achievements, and new goals. We wanted them to fall in love with us, or barring that, to desire us. "See how extraordinary we are, dammit!" we wanted to shout. "See how different we are from everybody else! Recognize us! Know our names! Pick us!"

Why shouldn't they take us up on what was sometimes an almost explicit offer? After all, we'd been doing our reading. John Updike told us that "[G]entle and knowing defloration had been understood by some of the younger, less married faculty gallants as an extracurricular service they were being salaried to perform." One of Philip Roth's heroes imagines lecturing to the students about "the undisclosable—the story of the professor's desire," where he makes clear that he finds "our classroom to be, in fact, the most suitable setting" for the "accounting of my erotic history." We knew it wasn't all fun and games. We'd read *Villette*, we'd read *The Prime of Miss Jean Brodie*, we'd read *Middlemarch*; hell, we'd read *Lolita*. It wasn't like this was something new.

Not only had we been reading; we'd been observing. Lots of professors had married their former students; the faculty wives we'd meet were often once graduate students themselves. That they now seemed to be given to typing and child-rearing, making sandwiches for parties to be devoured without appreciation by hordes of other women's grown children didn't make us envy them any less. They'd married the teacher. They'd won the prize. They'd have for their very own those wonderful figures who wove magnificent patterns of understanding out of indecipherable texts, who could impart to them the mysteries and sad beauty of the ages. (Occasionally it was male students who'd married female professors, but that was as rare as being assigned a book written by a living woman author in a modern novel course.) The accepted story was this: young women married the older men who'd held in their eyes the promise of knowledge and pleasure.

Except that it doesn't work that way. Marry the teacher, you end up with the person. The teacher doesn't belch or fart; the person does. The teacher doesn't get cranky if dinner is late, the teacher doesn't want to watch a rerun of *Ace Ventura, Pet Detective,* the teacher doesn't mispronounce the name of a fine wine, or embarrass you by not knowing that Bono is the lead singer for U2 and not the guy who was married to Cher. In *Down Among the Women,* by Fay Weldon, we meet a young girl intrigued by a man forty years her senior.

She is tickled by the thought of how much life this older gentleman has experienced. The narrator cautions us however that "It isn't her desire that is stirred, it is her imagination, but how is she to know this?" The point about the difference between desire and imagination is like the confusion between loving the profession and loving the professor.

We were smart enough to know better, but we didn't. All right, all right, enough with the "we." I was smart enough to know better, but I didn't. I thought that the closest I could get to being the teacher was loving the teacher; I thought that the closest I could get to playing school was playing doctor with somebody who taught school.

I wanted their attention and approval, not a better grade. I was pretty secure about being a good student; I wasn't secure about being pretty and a good student. I wanted a professor who would happily grade me on my life and recommend me for the highest award: himself. That these gentlemen were more or less interchangeable didn't strike me as odd at the time.

Thank God at one point I ended up taking a required class where there was a woman in the front of the room. The professor was amazing. She was charming, magnetic, funny, and wise. Intelligence and authority wafted around her, like perfume or scent; you could pick up a hint of it just from being near her, perceive it before she spoke or even looked in your direction. I leaned forward to hear her every word and wasn't conscious about whether or not my face was at a flattering angle. I sat in the front row without wondering whether I should cross my legs. I met her for coffee at eight o'clock in the morning with cornflakes in my hair, having run out of the dining hall to make our appointment on time. I looked at her with adoration, not thinking, "Boy, would I like to go home with her" but instead thinking, "Boy, would I like to do what she does for a living."

I believe—because I have seen it—that male professors can encourage, inspire, nurture, and support their women students without ever casting a shadow of inappropriate sexuality, and that the increasing number of women academics can do the same with the young men who pass through our offices. But it remains true that education, if it's done right, involves an intense and lasting link between two human beings. That link, however, doesn't have to be the first in a chain of mismatched sexual couplings we drag around through life.

That moment of connection can instead lead to what happens when we translate our desire into a love of the subject, or the text, or the way the light hits a four o'clock window in a November classroom.

🐜 44. *1976*

One of the first women tenured in the English Department is teaching Erica Jong's Fear of Flying. *The class has already been through all the usual contemporary writers—Mailer, Updike, Roth, and Cheever. A woman writer leads them into new territory. At the start of every class, this professor assigns a male student and a female student to give a personal response to the book under discussion. The female student says that she finds Jong's novel incredibly powerful as well as hysterically funny, and she is amazed at the honesty in the way it speaks to women's experiences. She loves Isadora Wing for both her strengths and insecurities, and focuses on the passage where Isadora unexpectedly gets her period in the middle of Paris and must duck-walk around until she finds a tampon. Then the male student gets up and expresses his outrage. "Reading," he objects, "is not a gendered experience." He insists that he, too, feels just as sympathetic with and connected to Isadora as he would to any E. L. Doctorow character. He bristles at the idea that*

Isadora's concerns are about being a "woman" and not simply "a human being." Jong's witty, satirical writing speaks to him directly. And as to the other issue, he snorts dismissively, "Do you actually think men don't know what happens to a woman's body every other month?"

🐾   45. *Conversations*

An impatient Tiger tells me I no longer have permission to weep about the boyfriend from another college who broke up with me:

"This is not the plague. This is not cancer, or epilepsy, or diabetes. This is heartbreak. You get over heartbreak. You get up, make the bed, and go to class. That's what you do. Make your bed. Eat some fruit. You are not an early victim of the black death. Don't act like you need to wear a black robe and ring a bell before you can walk down the hall."

🐾   46.

I loved the library, instantly and entirely. Inside that building, quiet as a church or a hospital, I could relax and look around without fear of reprimand. Palpably different from the judgmental stillness of the cathedral or the anxious hush of a sick-room, a contagious sense of safety filled the library's rooms. This sense of safety is what I remember best. I didn't mind being assigned a research paper. I learned how to use the huge and intimidating microfilm reader, which was sort of like learning how to operate heavy machinery designed by NASA. I spent hours roving in the stacks. Even during my first semester, I became desperately fond of interlibrary loan and regarded it as my passport to libraries in, for example, other galaxies. The weight of books calmed me; the feel of the paper under my fingertips as I turned the page grabbed and held me.

This pleasure was sharpened by the understanding that what I loved at that moment had been loaned to me. I could possess it fully but only temporarily—like life.

Eventually I decoded the processes whereby a regular person such as myself was permitted to have access to books usually reserved solely for use by Real Scholars. It was great: I felt like I was getting away with something. What I remember best, however, is that at that pocket-size, imitation-Tudor style English Department library, Sanborn House, tea and cookies could be bought for chump change at four o'clock every weekday afternoon. This was wonderful. The idea of eating in a library was as illicit as reading a novel during a dinner party—it seemed eccentric and (in some unspoken-rule-breaking way) marvelous. At other times, I would sneak in a bag of crackers and small squares of cheddar cheese, making absolutely sure that there were no crumbs left (my fear of library mice being strong and supported by powerful evidence). I was a devoted worker; my sin was, I believe, a venial one.

47. *Conversations*

Overheard at the Bull's Eye Bar; two faculty members, one female and young, one male and middle-aged, proving professors are human:

"You're fifty-one, fifty-two?"
"Yes, that's right, fifty-one."
"And the woman you're seeing, let me guess, she's thirty-seven or thirty-eight?"
"Amazing, how do you know?"

"And, let me guess again, you have kids and she doesn't?"

"Right."

"And she says she doesn't want any but I'm telling you, she's going to decide to want kids within three years."

"There, you're wrong, finally! She is so committed to her writing, she's not going to grieve over this childless thing. Besides, she says having my kids in her life will be the perfect compromise."

"Uh huh."

"What do you mean, 'uh huh'?"

"It isn't true. She's keeping her options open."

"She's not that kind of duplicitous creature."

"Wanna bet?"

"What are you, clairvoyant or just a pain in the ass?"

"Both."

48. *They Close the Library on the Weekend?*

Arming oneself with a visible dislike of sports is no way to approach Dartmouth. It's sort of like heading into the desert muttering, "But I'm very sun-sensitive" to which the only reply is "Why didn't you think of that before you embarked on this journey?" The lame answer: I just didn't realize. Where I grew up, *Lotto* was considered a big sport; men did not run unless someone in a unmarked car was chasing them. Women didn't run, ever.

There I am in 1975, hauling books to the library on this perfect autumn afternoon, ready to trade them in for the next batch, ready to make good on whatever efforts had sent me to this tiny town, ready to be the poster girl of a bona fide college student. I climb up the steps, get to the door of Baker, sacks full of weighty tomes across my shoulders like some medieval peddler. As I tug at the massive doors, even I can see (weak-armed and weak-shouldered as I am) that there is no movement. The doors are locked. How can this be? I am as puzzled as a character in the *Twilight Zone*. It's daylight; it's a weekend afternoon; there have been no reports of plague or riots; I am at an Ivy League school.

"Why the hell is the library closed?" I shout indignantly to some guys walking by.

"There's a football game," they shout back, laughing at my question. I figure they are kidding. I sit on the steps, and a few minutes later ask the same question to an older couple walking by. The yell back the same answer.

At that moment I discover I am not in the *Twilight Zone:* I'm in the *Outer Limits*. I am the Rogue Reader, the Stealth Student at a college that Shuts Down the Library During Home Football Games.

Fifteen years later, I am recounting this story to an appreciative group over cocktails at a swanky New York party (the only town where the word "swanky" still applies) and this tall dark-haired guy at my left shoulder is listening. He hears me get to the punchline— "And They Shut Down the Library During Home Football Games!" whereupon, as if on cue, everybody laughs out loud—except the tall man who says to me, with impeccable dignity, sophistication, timing, and a sly sense of James Bondian style, "And your point is?" and pauses. Then everybody laughs back at me.

The tall man (a graduate of Dartmouth, as you guessed) and I are friends, but we still clash over the issue of athletics. He thinks sports are good and tends to repeat that phrase in an argument— and not only because it is comprised of words with only one syllable. No, this guy works with words for a living and although he claims to have been an athletic type in his day, I've never seen him in a sweatshirt or wearing a terry cloth wristband, which makes me wonder if all those photographs of him on varsity teams are merely computer-generated.

But he loves this stuff, talks to me about scores and standing as if I had a clue what he meant, and expects me to support the college by cheering on its teams. My face still manages that grimace-like smile but I still just don't get it.

I did cheer for a Dartmouth team once. The Dartmouth women's basketball team played at UConn, and I was engaged by the game. I rooted for one side and then the other—my loyalties deeply and obviously divided to the point where those listening to me cheer for both sides suggested medication. These young women were, I knew, genuine scholar-athletes, and I liked the fact that the hyphenated phrase works in the order it does: *scholar* comes first. They clearly enjoyed the various parts of their lives, making it easy to commend them as role models. They seemed to be able, as so few of us can manage, to live in the moment: their focus is *this* game, *this* evening, *these* comrades, *these* moments as a student. But I was shockingly happy when Dartmouth gathered up points (or tossed points in, or racked them up, or whatever it is one does with points). It was exciting and fun to watch, so it became clear, even to me, that it must be a blast to play.

Not to worry: this did not make me purchase sneakers or do anything else drastic. But it did give me a sense of camaraderie with the tall guy.

🐜 49.

On the memo board for our dorm floor someone writes "John called."

Underneath someone else writes "Jesus wept."

50.

Rain and sleet drive against the one big window in our second-floor room. I hear the weather before I open my eyes and scrunch my feet down to the very bottom of the narrow bed. Nobody should have to get up, let alone walk across campus to a comp. lit. class on Ibsen and Strindberg, in this remorseless storm.

It's late October, cold and dank, and no tourists come to New Hampshire for the scenery now.

Iris remains so tidily asleep that she will barely need to adjust the sheets in order to neaten her side of the room. Her classes start at 10 A.M. Mine start at 8 A.M. In genuine bitterness, I try to remember why that seemed like a good idea when I was putting my schedule together at the end of last semester.

Oh, right. It's practically a required course for literature majors even though the actual concept of "required courses" has been replaced by a system whereby a student takes a number of classes grouped by discipline. Or something like that. My advisor, having no real knowledge of—and even less interest in—how the new system works, simply asserts that the comp. lit. class would be a fine choice.

My advisor teaches only in the late afternoon. He doesn't have to get out of bed this miserable morning in order to learn about *The Master Builder,* which is, anyway, a play whose title is really terribly easy to misstate when you're in a bad mood.

And I'm in a bad mood. I'm so exhausted I have trouble fumbling into my gray terrycloth robe; I feel like I'm trying to put on a space suit. I consider ditching the whole idea of clothing—why bother? After all, we're in an all-female hallway. Even though the dorm itself is coed, we do not share toilets or bathing facilities with the guys. Tiger once summed it up: "At least we do not have to gaze at pisscakes."

Plus, the bathroom is directly across from the room Iris and I share. On nights when we've gone to a concert, or a dance at the Afro-Am house next door, or Frat Row (also next door), it's great not to have to race wildly down the hall to pee away cheap wine, tequila sunrises, or—in one moment of unparalleled stupidity— peppermint schnapps. We can stagger the five feet from bed to loo without a map. Practically without a thought.

On those other nights, however, when one of us is in the room studying in the sepulchral calm of a veritable cloister, listening to those cheap, profligate concubines piss their educations away, it is hugely disheartening.

This morning I'm lucky. The place is as empty as church on a weekday. I'm the only one using the facilities, as my aunts used to call the bathroom. The orangey-brown walls, the florescent lights, the cold yellow tile provide an inhospitable atmosphere but at least I don't have to make small talk to the other eight inhabitants of our hall. At least I don't have to be cheerful. It's bad enough having to share a bathroom with seven other girls. Having to share one with six members of the chorus line for *Mary Poppins,* deliriously happy and whimsical and about to break into a synchronized swimming routine before breakfast, is intolerable.

I'm already in the shower when one of the Hummel figurines who lives in the next room waltzes in. Not that there's anything truly wrong with her. It's not her fault she looks like Queen of the Bulgarians; if I expect her to start yodeling any minute, that's *my* problem and not hers. The fragile compact of dorm life hinges on my being polite and her not taking offense. So even when she starts to hum the Carpenter's "We've Only Just Begun," I don't actually hurt her. I throw no dangerous objects in her direction. I don't whip out of the shower in all my blaspheming nakedness to hold her captive with my Lady Schick until the Campus Police show up with walkie-talkies and mace. I soap up and rinse, groping for the towel I left right outside the shower's door in order to maintain appropriate outhouse delicacy. Queen B. is even kind enough to hand me the edge of the towel.

When you consider the unscripted nature of this pantomime, you realize we're really doing a pretty good job of sharing a bathroom for two people who don't know each other.

I now have exactly fifteen minutes to dress and get myself to class. Indifferent to the fluttering promises of perhaps finding true love between Brown Hall and the basement of Dartmouth Hall where the class meets, I pull on jeans, wiggle into a soft woolly sweater, clomp into Frye boots (they can handle the rain) and take a half-hearted, amateurish swipe at my face with lipstick and mascara. I look more like a commando than a coed, but by racing across the Green I make it to class before the professor closes the heavy wooden door as he does every morning at 8 A.M. At 8 A.M. exactly. Before the last bell rings on the top of Baker library.

"No admission once the curtain is raised," Professor Fitz advised us on the very first day. "If you're late you might as well go to a penny arcade for amusement." Six feet tall and built like an appliance, he has blond hair cropped into a crewcut so severe he could be in the Marines. He is probably sixty years old and speaks with a half-English accent, sort of like David Nivens. "If you arrive late, you forfeit the opportunity to be protected by this small outpost of knowledge." He often refers to the official Latin motto of the college "Vox Clamantis in Deserto" ("a voice crying out in the wilderness") and adds "I am the vox, my dears, and THIS"—here he swings out his arm to encompass all that lies around him—"is the deserto."

You believe him, too.

(Years later, interviewing him for a story, I asked why he had stayed at Dartmouth for more than forty years; it had been his first and only job. I was expecting a long and absorbing explanation involving a sense of dedication and intellectual integrity. What he said—after two martinis—was this: "Why did I stay? Because of low self-esteem, darling, low self-esteem.")

I make it to class, wet and shivering, grab my usual seat in the front (easier to stay awake), open my book, and finally exhale. There are good reasons to be there on time apart from being exiled to the Deserto. Fitz's preamble is usually the best part of class. We hear about what the *New York Times* or *Boston Globe* printed in their morning editorials, or what NPR had reported just a few minutes ago. Fitz (or, as we called him amongst ourselves, "Fitzy") then magically connects the news of the day with what we'd been reading for class. Property, real estate, family hatreds, jealousy, covetousness, ambition, fear—they are at least as easily found in the daily papers as they are in Strindberg and Ibsen. Their past did not seem distant; their struggles remain the same as ours.

I like this teacher. I'm a little scared of him, not because he is demanding, which he is, but because I fear I won't live up to his high expectations. I've done well so far. My first paper got a B+ and we've only just taken the midterm.

Which, to my surprise, I see he has already graded. Blue books are piled on top of the rickety wooden desk, which he circles when talking and leans against when listening. He uses the blackboard capriciously; by the end of a 75-minute class, emblazoned at the front of the room, will be the following words: "hoax," "sadistic," "sublimate," "irreversible," and "courage." "Irreversible" is underlined twice.

He doesn't start today's class by telling us the news of the world. Instead he explains that he was disappointed by many of our midterms. "I asked you specific questions and you supplied me with general answers," he complains. He keeps his voice low and looks at us as if struck anew by our limited intelligence.

I'm beginning to regret my front-row seat because I can feel his reproach wash over me. Gnawing at my empty stomach is the memory of having gone with Iris to watch the film club showing of *Citizen Kane* when I should have been cramming for this exam. I shouldn't have convinced myself that because I love the plays, depressing as they are, I know how to analyze them.

"Some of you need to rethink your role as a student at this institution. There is no justification for some of the prodigiously tiresome writing on these pages. I am not a schoolmistress, cheaply appeased by the recitation of my own thoughts. I expect you to think for yourselves as well as to provide a critical perspective on texts you have carefully prepared." He sounds like the professor from last term's freshman seminar.

No sound from anyone.

"I will now read excerpts from a few of the better exams in order to provide you with examples of what is expected of you."

I have my head down now, hiding under my hair, scrunched into the chair the way I earlier scrunched into my bed, waiting to hear monumental arguments provided by those classmates more suited to the rigors of academic life.

Fitzy starts reading an essay on Ibsen's *Ghosts* and I'm thinking how I also wrote about hypocrisy, repressed sexuality, and the ambiguous position of the female servant. I'm thinking about how I will never have an original idea no matter how hard I try.

I'm doodling, as I always do, in the margins of my spiral notebook when it begins to soak in: it's *my* essay he's reading. I look up.

He has the front of the exam booklet folded back in an effort to keep it anonymous, but I see my scrawled notes on the inside jacket.

This is unbelievable. I wrote one of the exams he LIKES. I wrote a midterm he is using as an EXAMPLE of what other people should aim for; I am listening to a professor read MY words out loud not because they are funny or weird or dead wrong but because they are GOOD.

I am one of the good students.

After staring practically open-mouthed with wonder at Fitzy, I put my head back down and now doodle even more intently in the margin. I am hiding because I am blushing, which almost never happens, and because I am secretly grinning like a lunatic.

The morning is perfect.

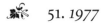 51. *1977*

(*Frat house. Afternoon. Untidy single bedroom, including unmade bed, unlit lamps, dirty coffee cups, full ashtrays, etc. Window with white blind drawn all the way down. Guy sits, unshaven, in white un-*

On the way to a Halloween frat party.

dershirt and shorts at a desk piled high with papers, wadded and un-wadded, and a manual typewriter. He opens what looks to be a third beer can—there are two open cans on the desk beside him).

Raising the can high with a flourish:

LARRY: Linda, this Bud's for you!

(Drinks deeply. Looks around the room slowly, as if deciding whether to do anything. There's a knock on the door.)

LARRY: Linda? LINDA? (*Yelling, he opens the door so wildly it bangs against the wall.*) DO YOU WANT COFFEE?

(Gina enters the room, walks past LARRY *and sits down on the one available chair.* LARRY *stays by the door staring at* GINA *with extreme disappointment on his face.)*

GINA: You're looking at me like I'm something you don't want to see in your backyard. Stop it. *(Pause)* That's better. And I would like coffee.

LARRY: I can't believe it. *(He closes the door and sits on the bed.)* I was sure it was her. I thought I caught a break.

GINA: Linda called me last night. She said you kept groaning into her telephone when she answered, then hanging up. I think that's illegal.

LARRY: I was not groaning, I was weeping. She doesn't know the difference between the two. That's the problem with that woman. *(Brightening.)* She knew it was me, though, didn't she? She recognized my voice even though I didn't really speak.

GINA: Which is not necessarily a compliment. She asked me to find out if you were okay because she didn't know what to do *(gesturing toward the chaos of the room)* and because you still don't have your own phone and she refuses to call the house, which I can understand since most of your brothers can't actually form letters yet in order to leave a message. Can I actually have coffee or was that just for Linda?

LARRY: Ask Hamster for coffee.

GINA: That guy next door still makes every single cup of coffee you drink?

LARRY: And Hamster hears every word through these walls. Yes. *(More loudly)* and grateful I am for every cup. *(lies down on the bed)*

GINA: That was one of the final straws for Linda, you know. (LARRY *looks up.*) Not the thin walls *(lowers her voice)* but that fact that you let that weirdo make you coffee every single day.

LARRY: Do you want coffee? Then ask him. If not, then change the subject or *(not with anger, but as if in explanation)*, you know, you can leave. You can tell Linda you came to see me just like she asked.

GINA: I'll deal with Linda on my own; she's my friend as well as your ex-girlfriend, remember. Put the beer away. *(Pause)* This place is something else. The roaches must be calling their friends from other towns to come over here. Don't you ever clean? *(as if in translation)* You know, like throw old food away? Tidy up? Don't you ever act your age . . . isn't your birthday like tomorrow?

LARRY: (slowly) Yep. *(Pause)* Twenty-two. Still fresh. *(with hope)* Not doing badly for my age?

GINA: Larry, tell me—look, let's talk about the way you get through the day.

LARRY: Question and answer? I like this part. *(Sitting up, straightening up slightly, as if going for an interview and as if he didn't mind being interviewed all that much)* Okay. Well, basically, I work on *(slight, pretentious shrug)* my book. *(He puts the beer down; he looks pleased with himself.)*

GINA: Hey, not bad. Sounds good when you put it that way.

LARRY: What do you mean "that way?" It's true!

GINA: *(Prompting)* What's the title of the book?

LARRY: *One Hundred and One New Elephant Jokes.*

GINA: Don't you think that slightly undercuts the "working on my book" line?

LARRY: At least I'm not working for a corporation . . .

GINA: There are worse things than working for a corporation—

LARRY: *(cutting in)* Like death by fire—

GINA: *(Looking at her friend for a moment)* Yeah, yeah, we all know you don't want to grow up to be your father, class of '57. Let's fast-forward through that since we've been over it for two years.

LARRY: *(again, proudly, playing the game)* I also spend time teaching Latin.

GINA: Say again?

LARRY: All right, tutoring Latin.

GINA: Want to know who tutors Latin, Larry? You and defrocked priests. What are you gonna do, put up those little signs with the flaps you rip off, put them up at the Hop and at the Village Green coffee shops saying, "Tired of working with those defrocked priests? Come and try a new approach to Classical Languages. Be taught by the author of the world famous text, *One Hundred and One* NEW—"

LARRY: *(Slumping back down, picking up the beer)* Thank you, thank you, friend of my soul. Receiver of my secrets. I also make decent grades. *(A knock on the door)*

GINA: But you don't make the coffee. *(Rises and exits. The door remains open and we hear a muffled exchange;* GINA *reenters, carrying two big mugs of coffee.)*

LARRY: I wanted to marry Linda. She is, as the song goes, the only one who can mend my heart.

GINA: *(between sips)* I don't want to encourage you, but I'm not sure what you mean . . .

LARRY: I mean that I am sure that I would love this woman for the rest of my life: She would give me beautiful children. It's like I can see the ghosts of these unborn children standing in front of me. I can see us spending our old age together sitting on a swing in the backyard.

GINA: *(quickly)* There are no such women. Not Linda, not anybody else. There are only such women in your head and on TV.

LARRY: *(dismissing her, eager to get on with his story)* No, no, you're really wrong. In another lifetime maybe we could have made it work. When she wouldn't have been in class with me, when she wouldn't have to see me except at the weekends. Maybe a couple of generations ago it would have been fine. If we had been at some 1945 victory party, it could have been fireworks and merry-go-rounds. I like the idea. Who knows?

GINA: Linda wouldn't have liked that idea at all, at all. She always told me that she felt like you were about to fall in love with somebody else. *(pause)* Like every one of your female classmates, for example.

LARRY: *(starts juggling balled-up wads of paper; he's good at it)* That's because I made the mistake of being honest with Linda when we were first going out. I told her that I was bored to death by one class because there wasn't anybody I could consider kissing; every group of people you deal with on a regular basis has to include one person you could imagine kissing or else it's a lost cause.

GINA: This is how you judge groups? Is there someone you can kiss?

LARRY: Not for real. *(stops juggling)* I meant just imagining, I never meant for real. She wanted to harness my imagination. *(speaking quietly and seriously now, putting an arm on* GINA*'s shoulder)* If I got a hard-on in my sleep she'd get jealous and wake me up.

GINA: *(turning away—very embarrassed)* Oh, come on . . .

LARRY: I'm serious, Gina. She would be subtle, but that was what she was doing. There Linda would be, poking me in the thigh or shaking my shoulder and asking whether I was having a nightmare. I guess I was breathing heavily, I don't know. She did it all the time. She wouldn't even let me be unfaithful while I was *unconscious. (Now he's pleading)* What could I do, after all? Gina, I was never actually unfaithful to Linda.

GINA: Meaning?

LARRY: I never slept with another woman while I was sleeping with her. Isn't that the textbook definition?

GINA: I don't know. *(as if puzzling this over for herself)* I don't know what "counts" as infidelity.

LARRY: Once or twice, maybe, a drink with an old girlfriend over Christmas break. A kiss good-bye. Lasting a little longer than necessary. But nothing else, nothing. I loved being with Linda. It was sort of like being in therapy except she did all the talking. It was much more relaxing.

GINA: But you never did justice to your relationship with Linda. Even after you moved in together you kept introducing her as your "friend." *(laughs)*

LARRY: *(defensive)* So?

GINA: When you were living together, I remember Linda sitting on the bed saying "Larry is my friend and this is our room" and laughing like hell. She wasn't your "friend." I am your "friend." A friend is somebody you grab a sandwich with at work. Or it's some girl you met on a road trip whose last name you don't remember. Linda was your "girlfriend" or "lover," or whatever word you want except for "friend." What was it she wanted that was so impossible to supply?

LARRY: *(embarrassed)* I hated stuff like holding her hand in public.

GINA: *(honestly baffled)* How could you possibly hate holding hands?

LARRY: Only in public. I don't even know if I should say this out loud because it's so stupid. I feel like I'm twelve years old. *(sits on the window sill;* GINA *now sits on the bed)* I never even admitted this to Linda: but I always wondered if there would be somebody else I could love just that little bit more. Somebody incredible, somebody once in a lifetime; this somebody would see me all domestic, holding hands with pretty Linda and I would lose her . . .

GINA: Life is not some kind of emotional "Let's Make a Deal" where you're always going for what's behind the curtain. Maybe you think Linda was never right for you because otherwise you wouldn't keep looking around this way—

LARRY: *(getting anxious, his voice rising)* Don't you see, that's just the point? Linda was that unknown other woman; she was somebody else's girlfriend I met at a beer-pong party—don't you remember? I looked across the room and it was like the goddamn scene from *West Side Story* when Tony starts singing "Maria." I went home from that party and I cried for an hour and a half; I loved her. I knew it, Jesus Christ, I knew it. *(absolutely in need of his friend's reassurance)* Remember? (GINA *nods)* I called you that night.

GINA: *(slowly, recalling)* I'd only just started going out with James and he wanted to know whether my guy friends always called in the middle to the night. You know, now that I'm remembering this, I remember *(getting angry slightly)* that we had a fight about that because he accused me of having a crush on you . . . I had to talk to him for about four hours, you bastard. Anyway . . . so what changed, Larry? What changed??

LARRY: *(Pause)* I wasn't resilient to *(looking for the right word)* familiarity—that was it. She would cry straight at me sometimes, look into my eyes and sob and there was nothing I could do. I used to say inside my head, "Go away, go away, go away."

GINA: I'm listening. I have nothing to say yet. Go on.

LARRY: (pacing) You see, I couldn't *do anything. (impatiently)* And she wanted *anything. (Pause; goes to window and looks out)*

GINA: And now?

LARRY: But now? I write letter after letter, maybe a hundred pages in the last week, I swear to God, and I rip the pieces up. If I put all this stuff down in writing then it's like a contract I'll have to live up to for the rest of my life and I refuse . . . *(Pause)* As much as I can love anybody, I know that I love her.

GINA: Let's sum up your argument: men are selfish and women want too much?

LARRY: I don't know. I wonder whether it's me. You know me. *(Sits next to her, speaks very quietly)* What do you think?

GINA: *(Pauses, then lightly)* You know, Linda and I, when you two were living together, we used to sometimes talk about, trade different perspectives on you, trade these things to get to know you like the way astronomers would share information about different galaxies . . . What is it doing *now?* Is it condensing? Will it remain a swirling mass of gasses or become a solar system?

LARRY: What did she say? Do you still talk about me like that?

GINA: *(very seriously)* I had to stop because Linda started taking my words for your words.

LARRY: You speak better than I do.

GINA: Linda called me to come and to see how you are, but I wanted to talk to you about the other stuff—school, writing, your birthday. She's only part of it. She's the excuse. You know that.

LARRY: I don't know that at all. Shit.

GINA: I was thinking about when you stole Fat Johnny's skates on your birthday. Remember?

LARRY: I don't remember that.

GINA: You told me this story right when we first met. You liked some girl and there was a fat kid who had great skates and you didn't have any. So you took the skates out of Fat Johnny's locker and went to the playground and skated all the way the hell around the playground, doing all sorts of stunts and getting this girl's attention.

LARRY: Tammy.

GINA: What?

LARRY: *(now engaged in the story)* The girl. Her name was Tammy. Tammy McCord. I called her "The Face" but that was because I liked her.

GINA: Yeah, well, you got The Face's attention all right but then out comes the fat kid and starts screaming "thief, thief. . . ."

LARRY: *(smiling)* I actually and truly skated circles around him until the gym teacher—who was the biggest thing I'd ever seen alive—came out and picked me up off the ground and took the skates off my two feet. While holding me up. I walked in my socks to the principal's office.

GINA: One day you were saying something about knowing that you deserved more than you get; it was at some point when you were mad about a C on a paper or not getting some tutoring job; you were a better skater than this kid and he got the skates; you thought this girl and you would be great together but she was never going to look at you if you just acted like you always did.

LARRY: So?

GINA: You said that the trouble was, when you got something, you weren't sure that somebody else who didn't get it might have deserved it more.

LARRY: When you say it it's all so clear. When I try to explain something like this to Linda it would come out like in Martian or something—*(makes indistinct noise)* I can't say it.

GINA: So I'm supposed to act as your interpreter? You're the one who does interpretations.

LARRY: But when I speak I sound like a sonofabitch; I sound like some creep from a woman's magazine. When I was alone, I would read the copies of *Mademoiselle,* she would sneak into the apartment—and there were always these short stories about guys who couldn't "give of themselves" or whatever ridiculous language you people use and I would want to stick my finger in a socket, you know what I mean, because the worst guys always said things that I half thought I could say, or have said to women in the past, and then I started to think that maybe these stories were written by old girlfriends of mine who changed their names after we stopped going out—

GINA: That sounds pretty drastic—

LARRY: Yeah, but, otherwise it just makes us all, all men, sound the same, exactly the same. It must be like women feel when they see a picture that's just tits or some other piece of anatomy: if you take this thing out of context, it could belong to anybody. . . .

GINA: Maybe once or twice in your life a woman you think is the most terrific thing in the room comes up to you and you have a decent conversation and she seems interested in you, seems to actually like you. Right?

LARRY: Okay . . .

GINA: So you shouldn't then say something like, "you wait here and I'll be back in a little while as soon as I make a quick tour of the neighboring parties just to make sure there isn't somebody I like better." Because then you'll be right, you won't deserve her. So you'll make yourself a bastard immediately and then you can lose respect for her for falling for a bastard like you.

LARRY: Why do you know this stuff?

GINA: Because I can imagine doing everything that you do, I really can. I decide not to do it; life is too short. I sleep next to a wonderful guy almost every night. It seems a fair deal. Not perfect but fair. "Fair" as in "just," not as in no good.

LARRY: You know what I want for my birthday?

GINA: Skates?

LARRY: I want a coffee machine.

GINA: Okay. What else?

LARRY: Will you call Linda for me?

GINA: No. Next?

LARRY: I want a cake with a candle for each year; not all this adult crap of a few representative candles. One for the year I was eight, one for the year I was eighteen—all the years. They all count. There must be something symbolic in candles; and I haven't had a cake with candles since I was fourteen.

GINA: I've got a lot to do.

LARRY: The candles aren't hard to find. The little candy store at the corner has them.

GINA: You checked?

(LARRY *nods.*)

   52.

Elise from the Bronx was more comfortable with the word "Black" than "African-American." She came of age (insofar as thirteen is "of age") when the phrases "Black is Beautiful" and "Black Power"

had an impact. With four older sisters who adored her but were merciless in their teasing, Elise was the baby of the family who knew she could get her way by being smart, cute, and endearing. Not to mention that early in life, she also developed the skills of thinking through effective emotional and intellectual strategies tailored to both the situation and individuals involved.

She played to win. Elise's sport was field hockey. The posh Catholic girls' school for which she had played four years of varsity was bereft at the loss of their star. Field hockey was one of the best parts of Elise's life.

As she always said, "It's the only way a Black woman with a stick can run after a white woman and not get arrested."

 ## 53. *1977*

(a parody by Brooks Clark—and entirely representative of what student poets were writing)

"Coffee at the Hop Snack Bar."

We shambled across a starry plain
That day—you and I, brotherless.
With the retrievers and their sa
> l
>> i
>>> v
>>>> a-soaked
Tennis balls: suns of frosty innocence.

A rose pricked the rainbow
When you told me I was lonely.

A note on the candy machine said,
  "20 cents John Bussey, WDCR."
I am surrounded here, as I sip my coffee.
Without a CAT cap.

Without a sleeveless vest.
Without a nickname like "Pus"
    or "Glasseater" on my back.
I am in clogs . . . am I different?

The dog nips at my donut.
Why do people butt in line?

🐝 54. *From my journal, 1977*

Perhaps I'm not a "proper scholar" really—there's still something in me that feels fraudulent. Maybe I should be doing more "serious academic" work. Then again, if I can't write either of those phrases without using quotations marks, maybe I'm thinking about them the wrong way.

Today I got up the courage to ask the professor a question I had been wanting to ask her since the very beginning of the semester: did I speak too much in class? I always get a kick out of her questions and my hand shoots up like I'm trying to get the attention of a game show host. I feel ridiculous even though I know I'm not full of shit—I think about all this stuff on my own time and that's why I'm in the damn class to start with—but I'm afraid it was starting to seem like I was a stray cat trying to follow her home. I'm hoping her answer was as honest as it sounded. She seemed astonished by the very question and reassured me that it wasn't the case. "The class," she suggested, "would probably tell you to shut up if you just hogged the time or your comments went on too long." She added "you've never said anything stupid and there's no reason to be embarrassed about being both curious and ambitious" which felt like a compliment.

Sort of.

I did feel a little funny about the word "ambitious" because wanting to succeed seems so ruthless, and selfish, and frankly pretty bitchy. I admitted this to her because otherwise I knew not saying it would keep me up all night. She got all serious, stopped putting her papers into her briefcase which is what she had been doing, and looked me right in the eyes: "Don't stand there and tell me you don't care whether or not you succeed. We all tell students that they should want to learn for the sake of learning but that's not all there is. You might sit in this class for the pure joy of it"—*and she laughed because she was sort of kidding around*—"but reading and taking notes is not an end in itself. You have to make the ideas your own. And I suspect that for Gina, making something your own will always involve talking about it."

From the overstuffed shelf behind her, she grabbed a copy of a paperback book. "Here, keep this. It's Virginia Woolf's essay, A Room of One's Own."

I took it to my room as if I were a shoplifter and read it all at once. Woolf talks about how she was barred from entering even the libraries at the great universities of England around the turn of the century. She's walking along the paths at "Oxbridge" university when she's yelled at by the guard at the gate. Not surprisingly, she begins considering the nature of exclusion. Here is one of the century's greatest authors and she's not allowed to go into a university library because the male students and scholars cannot bear to be disturbed by a woman—and they find women essentially disturbing. Woolf thinks "how unpleasant it is to be locked out." But it then occurs to her "how it is worse perhaps to be locked in."

Woolf wonders about the "safety and prosperity of the one sex and of the poverty and insecurity of the other and of the effect of tradition and of the lack of tradition" on the minds of young people who inherit the belief that one group is better than the other. To be denied access to a system is bad but it is nevertheless infinitely preferable to being fixed in place and locked into the system. Reading Woolf that day was another providential moment for me. Maybe my ambition would be about discovering that scary wizards are just guys with levers who control smoke and mirrors. Maybe after the initial surprise wears off, you discover that you have options: you can laugh about it, you can learn how to do it yourself, or you can change it.

In other words, clear away the dust and clouds of your own fears and worries and what you have is: freedom.

55. Conversations

A male friend leaving for graduate school wants to have one last fling with his former lover. "It will be nice to make love because we'll never see each other again."

"*Because?*" She gives him a familiar look of affection and impatience combined. "*Because* we'll never see each other again? You could have *at least* said 'despite the fact' that we'll never see each other again—"

56. *1977*

This is a secret love story that has only a little bit to do with secrets and slightly less to do with love. It's about heading through the night with the radio on, moving a big old car toward another country, and only incidentally a story about crossing borders, or erasing boundaries.

He was a year ahead of me and had ushered me into the ways of the college when I first arrived, helping me choose the best professors, encouraging me to learn the words to the songs and the ways of this particular world. Protective of me and defensive of the place, he had a tough position to play.

Even though we had known each other for years, we knew only those things one knows from classes and meetings; we knew one another casually and intimately at the same time. I knew how much milk to put in his coffee, for example, and he knew I didn't like to call him at his fraternity house for fear of hearing one of the brothers bellow my name up the stairs to him, but I didn't know whether he snored and he didn't know whether I slept in a T-shirt, a nightgown, or nothing at all.

I had occasionally tousled his hair as I passed by him, half reading in the library, and he bought me flowers on my birthday once when everyone else seemed to have forgotten. Knocking on his door late one night, ignoring the noise, I cried to him over the loss of some other man, and he held me at arm's length. And I wondered whether to focus on the fact that I was held, or that I was held at a distance.

We had no anniversaries to share or reason to kiss except to say hello or good-bye after the absence of a vacation, a term away, or parting before a major holiday. We did not kiss. We didn't date. We were friends.

We liked each other, and looked forward to random meetings at the snack bar where we both worked. We were competitive, and each hoped the other would do very well but maybe not better, wincing slightly at being given an A- if the other received an A, and yet we were happy for each other's happinesses: we became better friends after he got a girlfriend at another college because we were positioned on a level playing field. I smiled more deeply into his eyes, and he permitted himself the occasional compliment about my clothes or expression.

His relationship made everything that much easier. He was able to say "My girlfriend and I . . ." in reply to a phrase that included "My boyfriend and I." It was easier for me to hear the possessiveness in the words "my girlfriend" than it had been for me to hear a series of names that I had to memorize and keep steady in my head, like a little ensemble of beauty queens waltzing through my imagination. I was fond of his girlfriend. I wouldn't have believed that one of the reasons I liked her was because I felt as if I had a reasonable edge. The girlfriend was adorable but not quick; she was devoted, but lacked the appeal of independence.

But of course the girlfriend was amply compensated: she knew that my friend snored only when he'd had too much to drink, and only she knew how often he had too much to drink. He'd drink a lot, for example, when the four of us went to the Bull's Eye. She was grateful for his warmth in her bed every night, having loved him for more than two years and having known him for three; he and her sister graduated the same year from a small high school in Rhode Island. She decided not to worry about me, I think, and so made a point of encouraging us all to enjoy one another's company.

She liked me and seemed mildly attracted to my boyfriend, making it easier for them to talk; if paired off by default in a social situation or by a seating arrangement, they were not unhappy. Older by two years or so, handsome, witty, and relaxed into his well-deserved sense of pleasure at being in graduate school in Boston, my boyfriend appreciated women with the same delight as he appreciated expensive and contraband cigars: they had been out of reach when he was an undergraduate and would not now pass him by without his admiration.

We were all right, you see, up to a point.

It was late April, the day of the first big spring picnic that a bunch of us threw before the real parties started at the end of the term. There was still some sneaky snow on the ground, in the shadows, but there were games, lakes, lunches, drinks, laughter, conversation, all making up for the cold. Friendly dogs buzzed knee-high like small planes, wheeling and spinning around people they had never met, confident of approval. The groomed and polished woods by the river sang with invented warmth, and as groups arrived the others made room, expanding into the shade or the sun. My boyfriend arrived early, packing a picnic basket full of shareable goods: pâté, wine, exotic cheeses, and British biscuits. We each held one handle, carrying the burden between us. The other two arrived later with a cooler full of imported beer in each hand, laughing at the fact that they had to pack them in paper bags in order to disguise it from those acquaintances who had been circling around the bottles like vultures around a kill.

I sat next to my friend. Wearing a striped T-shirt and shorts, his battered Converse sneakers made him look even more like a cartoon character than usual. Long fingers were wrapped around a cold beer. Dark hair, collar length, just too long or just right, depending where you stood and I was standing right next to him. *I'm sitting too close to him. Will this will make everybody nervous?* I didn't move.

I've been afraid that I'd been overdoing it lately, that I'd been calling too much or leaving too many messages on his door, telling him too many stories and laughing too hard at his jokes. Drinking a glass of wine (beer was like skiing, something I knew everybody else liked but the pleasures of which escaped me) and smiling I was quiet. *His jokes are a narcotic to me, making the day go faster and my own existence brighter, and I need to tell him what happens to me everyday. Increasingly he's become the receiver of my imaginary conversations;*

the running commentary of the daily routine is directed toward him.
Maybe I thought something simpler: *What happens when you try
to be friends with somebody you find attractive? Can a woman and a
man be just friends or is that idea just a joke?*

When I didn't see him and he hadn't returned my phone calls for
a few days after the picnic, I started to worry. I stopped him on the
way into the library one night and, touching his arm just briefly,
asked him whether he was pissed off at me or annoyed or upset or
anything. He looked genuinely and welcomingly horrified; his eyes
widened and he said no, no, why did I think that? I told him about
the not-returned calls and he said that if he didn't call back right
away it was only because he was busy, I shouldn't think that I'd
done anything to provoke him—and then he said "Let's go. We've
been in this hick town too long. Cabin fever, stir-crazy early spring:
Let's blow this taco stand."

The 1967 Monte Carlo, always parked illegally, waited for action
behind the frat house. We got in and headed north. The signs
for towns in northern New Hampshire got brighter as the sun
started to set, took on that luminescent quality of unearthly color
so that they seemed to shine with their own odd brilliance, white
and green in unfamiliar markings. The car had a tape deck, a pe-
culiar piece of luck or else something stolen and installed by a
rogue cousin in Providence, and we listened to Steely Dan and
Bruce Springsteen and Patti Smith. I sang loudly and off-key but
I knew all the words and with the back windows down to blow
the smoke out of the car and the volume turned up you could
hardly tell I was way off the mark. He had a voice like traffic, rough
and low, and he knew all the words, too. The car had those long
slick bench seats and before we were at the border I'd dared myself to slide over, tucking myself under the long arm he had out-
stretched across the back. He didn't seem to notice. We kept
singing, looking for luck and signals in the songs. We felt like en-

gines that had lost their driving wheels, we knew that the door was open but the ride wasn't free, and we knew that the night belonged to lovers.

We sang so that we didn't have to speak, and we didn't want to speak because anything we would have said as the white lines moved faster beneath the dark wheels we would have regretted later. It was simple between us, but that didn't mean it was easy. Like knotted string, confused desire complicates what is simple.

At the Canadian border, we told the skeptical but lazy guard that we were going to look at graduate schools the next day, that we had interviews, that we were engaged. He didn't ask questions, which in a way was too bad: the fiction we'd created was an alternative universe, a virtual relationship, a life we could have been living except for the fact that we weren't.

We went looking for a place to eat, walking through the cold clear streets of brightly lit Montreal, a city awake after dark, just before midnight. He started singing "Mac the Knife," but using only the first line of the song, singing the same words over and over again even though he followed the tune. "When the shark bites, oh the shark bites, and that shark bites, see the shark bites. . . ." We laughed, and I put my thumb into the belt loop over his hip, feeling a slight limp in his walk from a hockey accident the winter before. We found a Kosher delicatessen and ate huge smoked-meat sandwiches, sharp pickles, and knishes that steamed when you broke them open. We sat at the counter, looking at each other out of the corners of our eyes, and talked to the waitresses in bad French, continuing the fiction we started at the border. We told them we were getting married in June and that we were both applying to graduate school at McGill. They told us which neighborhoods would suit us best. They giggled, conspirators in our elopement plans, and poured coffee into our cups as if it represented their good wishes. We said good-night to them around 2 A.M. and walked into the now chest-clenching cold of a star-filled night.

We knew our options. We knew there were hotels, we knew there was the Monte Carlo with its bedroom-sized seats. We knew there was the ease of walking hip to hip, despite the difference in height. And we knew it wouldn't work. Not when we had to face each other in the library, at work, at the Bull's Eye's long tables. Not when we still needed to talk about classes, and plans, and a future that included other people.

And so we began the drive back.

It was dawn when the college appeared, Main Street scrubbed white and just waking up. We sat in the car for a few minutes. I intended to leave abruptly, say good-night and go, but instead I sat. I was afraid he wanted me to leave quickly; I thought of asking him to drive around a little more but I knew I couldn't. So we sat and I moved, half-consciously, toward him. There was no music now.

He asked, expressionless, "You staying or going?"

Once said, the texture of the air changed, a shift in the cogs of our working together, something unlocking and then quickly relocking in ourselves. I reached over to put my hand on his and he covered it with both his hands, raised it to his warm mouth and kissed me, on the inside of my palm, briefly. There was no better time to go.

I knew, and he knew, I couldn't have been his girlfriend, couldn't have been softly sweet or constantly agreeable any more than I could have made little quilted pillows or hit a brilliant backhand; I could not do these things. My past was too filled with the tensions of choice to let myself be thinned, like paint, in order to be applied more easily to him. He couldn't have given up skiing and hockey, wouldn't have wanted to compete all day at school and come home only to continue the battle, exhilarating as it was.

Were we linked by destiny or by circumstance? We had the college in common, but we were afraid to find out if there was more. The friendship had to be more enduring, we figured, than any other version of ourselves.

But I wonder now whether that was true.

The friendship buckled, finally, under marriages and kids and distance and these grown-up lives of ours; I don't know where he lives or what he thinks about. And yet there was something put away during that night trip up north, something in self-storage, kept from the wear-and-tear of everyday life, still the edges of it sharp and clear.

 57.

Alumni would cluster in the lobby of the venerable Hanover Inn. There was much good humor to be restored with much slapping of back and bottom. Their wives, arrayed in the dark pine-green turtlenecks and knife-pleated skirts that betrayed their origins and their aging knees, stood by anxiously willing to please. One by one they were brought into the circle and introduced by the nicknames they continued to use: Bud met Mickie, Snapper met Penny, Chip met Suki, and Dinkie met Duckie. These people ran multinational corporations under their family names but preserved their individuality, as they saw it, by using the intimate form of address they used twenty, forty, for some with enormous courage, sixty years ago when they ran the campus. Someone would comment on the death of a classmate and someone would make a joke and they would laugh falsely and quickly, then talk of something else. They only had three days in town, after all, and were only too aware of their own mortality.

🐜 58.

My terror of airplanes might well have started the afternoon I left for the London Study Abroad program in 1977. This was by far the biggest trip anybody in my family had taken since they fled Sicily in 1909.

Well, that's not strictly true; my older brother had traveled much of the world by himself, but you must remember that he was Older and a Boy so I could hardly use him as a role model.

It's also true that my father got shipped off to bomb the enemy, but he hardly enjoyed the trip and didn't like planes any more than I did.

Let's narrow it down to say that women in my family never went anywhere beyond the reaches of the clothesline. I left for London weighed down with amulets and various religious paraphernalia to guarantee a safe trip. I had one or two rosaries, assorted rabbits' feet, notes of support, a lucky necklace, and a hardcover copy of *Gravity's Rainbow*. Other wiser or more experienced students carried only sleeping bags, paperbacks, and backpacks. We choose our own baggage, I have since learned, but I wasn't aware of that in 1977. I took everything with me because I had no idea what to expect.

There was a storm the afternoon of my departure from JFK that would have made the three witches from Macbeth feel perfectly at home. The runway was flooded and I considered escaping when the flight attendant had her back turned. Then I remembered that my roommate had already put in for a single and that none of the good classes would be open any longer; I was stuck in Study Abroad mode. I tried to focus on details because I was terrified by the step I was taking; I had finished my sophomore year in Hanover finally feeling comfortable and here I was abandoning that (finally) cozy environment to head into the unknown.

Along with the amulets, I carried the piece of paper from the Study Abroad office to reassure myself that this was all perfectly normal, but there were elements I found less than reassuring in this document. They included, for example, a list of suggested resources sent by the residence hall at University College, London, where I would be spending the next six months.

One of the items indicated that I should pack a "travel rug" for the room. Travel rug? I thought maybe I was supposed to roll up a piece of indoor/outdoor carpeting and drag it across the Atlantic. I had no idea that it meant I ought to bring a light blanket. I figured that I wouldn't need the suggested and mysterious "rucksack" because I didn't have a ruck on me. I was too embarrassed to ask what these words meant since they seemed self-explanatory to everyone but me. At that point in my life, I was wary of seeming as unsophisticated as I actually was.

The ultimate result of this, not surprisingly, was that I was left with a great many unanswered questions. And without a light blanket.

It's not like I thought I was going to the *moon*. After all, I knew people who had returned from London saying things like "lift" instead of "elevator" and talking about girls with "ginger-coloured hair" (you could practically hear them add the silent "u") instead of red-heads. One girl went into raptures about "chocky-bikkies" and another sang virtually orgasmic arias about the pleasures you could find by merely "chatting up" an Englishman. Clueless as I was about any exact translations of these terms, it all sounded good to me. My imagination was captured by the idea of myself standing on the very spot in the alley where Marlowe was stabbed to death; I loved the thought of going to the RSC and The National Theatre since these were places I'd actually heard of or researched for English papers. I wanted to see The Old Curiosity Shop. I pictured myself drinking tea and making charming conversation with my British betters. I thought of thatched cottages and delightfully gothic garrets. I thought of intimate yet high-powered seminars full of stunningly intelligent men and women my own age. I pictured myself as perfectly at ease.

Pictures lie. When I arrived in London the first thing I realized was that I had no idea how to handle the currency. I hailed a cab at Victoria Station and asked the driver if the fare to Tottenham Court Road would be less than a pound because I had more one pound notes than anything else. I was enormously relieved when he said yes, but was terrified the next moment as I saw him roll what I could only imagine was an enormous joint: he was certainly rolling something. I never knew anyone who actually made their own cigarettes.

So there I was, thinking I'm going to get busted for being in this guy's cab, or that at the very least he's going to swerve into oncoming traffic because all the other cars were clearly being driven by women and dogs. When the cab deposited me at the hall of residence, I was panic stricken. It was a blank concrete building of fifteen stories or more, and I was one of about three people in the place. I felt like Scrooge when he's left at school as a child because his father hates him.

I dragged my suitcases to the elevator, already wondering why on earth I'd brought books with me since I was only going to have to cart them back again. I was alone in a endlessly long hallway, and the first night there I wrote minute by minute in a notebook about my foolishness in leaving Hanover, about my belief that if there were a fire in this building a fifth-floor descent onto concrete was my only fate, about the fact that London looked about as quaint as Flatbush.

I heard people laughing from the street below and it struck me as unbelievably odd that for everybody else it was simply Tuesday night. I remember leaving the light on when I went to sleep and feeling about four years old. So much for sophistication.

Afraid that everybody I left at home would be either married or dead before I could make it back in March, I waited for mail as if I were a prisoner waiting for a pardon from the governor. When I didn't hear from him on the first day, I called my boyfriend collect. He was comforting. Figuring that what worked once would work twice, I called him an hour later. He was less comforting. When I called him a third time that day he told me that he couldn't afford my emotional trauma and suggested I go to a movie. It was not what I wanted to hear. He told me that he was disappointed in my lack of independence and the loss of what he called my adventurous spirit. I didn't call again for a while. I wrote letters on blue airmail stationery that I had the good sense not to mail. (Later on in my stay that measure of self-protective good sense would desert me, causing a great deal of wincing in anticipation of the week's delayed response. But that's another story.)

Classes at UCL would start at the beginning of the next week, and I knew that more students from Dartmouth would arrive over the weekend. I had decided to come early to London because I thought that after acclimating to Hanover I could make myself at home anywhere, figuring that I did indeed have an adventurous spirit, as long as I knew the territory. I knew I was out of my league on all levels when I went to buy myself a ham sandwich and figured I would get a version of the overstuffed Peter Christian's special. I was handed exactly one piece of flaccid ham between two slices of white bread smeared with butter. If I'd been keeping *kosher* I could hardly have been more appalled by this concoction. I was forced to admit how spoiled I was.

Other friends had spent time hiking through the rain forest, and one girl in our dorm had arrived fresh from spending three years in a small African village. Surely I could make it in a land that spoke my native tongue? Why was I so unprepared for the differences I found?

I decided to go for a walk. I walked to the law courts and admired the buildings. I walked down the Strand and went into bookstores afraid that someone would want me to buy something, but nobody even asked if I needed help. I walked to St. Paul's and to the HMS Discovery and to Big Ben. At least I was thoroughly exhausted by the time I went back to Ramsey Hall and could sleep without wondering every fifteen minutes what time it was "at home," and wondering what people were eating at Thayer Hall while I was eating Toad-in-the-Hole. (It would be a month before I discovered fish and chips.) During those first days, I groped around as if I were exploring a dark cave, not realizing that I carried a light with me even though I had packed badly.

The fourth or fifth day there, it poured for the first time since my arrival and that made me feel a little better; it was, after all, what I had expected all along. It was a foggy day in London town. Being a girl who knew her Cole Porter, I figured that for me at least the British Museum would not have lost all its charm. After all, I'd never seen it. A short walk down Tottenham Court Road, and I was immediately thrilled by the entrance to the museum because there was no admission price. In New York, I always forked over the suggested donation at the Met and I was prepared to do the same here. Being told that I could just walk in made me feel welcome in an entirely new way. I knew about museums and I immediately started searching for a place where I could buy a cup of coffee when I was stopped short by an illuminated manuscript of *The Canterbury Tales.*

Having witnessed Professor Alan Gaylord's recital of Chaucer's "The Miller's Tale" the year before, my attention was finally, wonderfully, and fully engaged by something outside myself. "Smalle birds Maken Melodye" I read, and my eyes filled with tears. This wasn't like anything I'd ever seen at home, not even from doing research with rare books or in the closed stacks. This was *Something Else,* with a history longer than anything I could imagine. People had looked at this manuscript before it became required reading, and now I was part of that history just by walking into this beautiful building for free. These lusciously magnificent pages weren't hidden away in some small room for the exclusive and fetishistic gaze of serious scholars but were instead right there on the ground floor. Suddenly it felt as if there were enough of *everything* to go around. I knew, with smiling relief, that I wouldn't have to be too scared to cross the Atlantic anymore. I'd found a place of safety. If this manuscript could be safe here, then so could I.

Within a month, I'd seen twelve plays, made good friends, fallen in love, and danced with Albert Finney at the National Theater's production of the Passion Plays. I'd taken classes with Randolph Quirk and knew more about the English civil war than I knew about the American one. With my A–Z (I always insisted on—and still say—"zee" and not "zed") under my arm I made my way all over the city that was, later on, to become home for three years.

Taking wing in London.

🐝 59.

While in London for that junior year, I earned money doing odd research jobs for the British Broadcasting Company. At a party (I always went to parties in those days because it meant free food), a producer I'd only just met asked me to appear on a TV show that was a sort-of grown-up version of College Bowl. It was called (I'm not kidding) "Mastermind."

You—the contestant—sat under a spotlight on a stage and an announcer fired questions at you concerning a special subject and what was vaguely titled "general knowledge." You had to answer as many questions as you could within the space of three minutes. If you didn't know the answer, you had to say "pass" because you risked losing points with an incorrect response—sort of like particularly demonic and public SATs. This producer explained—as I

stuffed myself with sandwiches—that the show had been syndi-
cated in seven or eight countries but the show never made it to the
States. Would I consider, he asked, acting as the official American
contestant?

I had never seen the program, but my British boyfriend of the moment had and he whispered that I shouldn't even consider such a
thing. He said, and I quote: "You'll look silly." That, of course, made
my decision for me. I agreed to be part of the show.

Then I actually watched the terrible televised ritual and was unnerved. I chose the life and works of the playwright Tennessee
Williams as my special subject. I crammed, memorized, and sweated
through even the most obscure plays and short stories. The boyfriend merely gloated. On the day of the taping, I had a remarkably
bad cold, a runny nose, and red eyes. I was fuzzy on cough syrup
and mad at the boyfriend who had refused to accompany me.

Shockingly, I did all right on the Williams material, but when it
came to "general knowledge," I knew almost none of the questions
they asked, many of which had to do with the United States. Despite my fancy education, I was horrifyingly ignorant. I could not
name all the states run through by the Mason-Dixon Line. I did
not know the highest point in Utah; I didn't know Utah had a high
point. I did not know the estimated population of Atlanta.

The audience members, five hundred strong, were holding their
breath in appalled silence as I kept saying "pass" over and over
again. In the back of my mind, I was taunting myself in my evil
boyfriend's voice: "See? What do you know? Where's your knowledge now?" I was miserable. Finally, the announcer, no doubt out
of sheer pity, asked me one glorious question: "What kind of ani-
mal is a guppy?" and I screamed out, "IT'S A FISH!"

There was applause like you never heard. You'd think I just scored a touchdown, hit the high note, and discovered gold all at once. Clearly the members of the audience were simply so relieved that I got one right, even just one, they forgave me everything. They whistled, they stamped their feet; I didn't look silly to them, although I certainly looked like somebody who beat the odds and had extra help on exams.

I discovered at that moment that anything worth doing was worth doing, period—worth doing well if you could, or doing poorly if you couldn't do better, as long as it got done with enthusiasm. Taking a risk is an experience. It will be a test of yourself; it can become the beginning of a story. As far as I can tell we only get to go through life once. But if we do it right, once is enough.

60. *Conversations*

Having fallen wildly in love with a medical student almost as soon as I stepped off the plane in London, I didn't know what to do about ending my relationship with the guy from Dartmouth I'd been seeing before I left. A sophisticated friend from the U.K. explained why I was permitted to break up with the home-based boyfriend even though he and I had spent all this time practically living in each other's rooms and taking the same classes. In her clipped English tones she explained, "Propinquity is a poor basis for life-long passion. Just because you brush up against somebody in the dark a few times doesn't mean you have to vow to love them forever."

🐜 **61.**

The girl woke up and looked around her. Not for a moment, not even in sleep, had she forgotten where she was or who she was with.

She was in Paris, it was Christmas, and she was alone, inside her dark hair, inside the foreign blankets, against the once sterile, now wrinkled white sheets that she wrapped like a cocoon around herself, covering her bare skin. There was a man, it was true, in the next bed, also swathed in white sheets and grey wool. A man, almost snoring, a man with a beard and wide shoulders and a well-respected presence, but a man with whom she would not sleep. She held him, brushed crumbs out of the beard, made love to him. But to sleep next to him was suffocating and the few hours she had tried the first night sent her to dreams about floods and nightmares about dying birds. Since then she had taken the small cot and curled herself into a conch shell of hair and sheets and blankets and slept dreamlessly.

But this morning she woke early and studied his face—her mouth slightly open and almost pouting. He looked warm and inviting. She remembered the feel of him around her, like a big pillow, supple to her movements, responsive even in sleep. Pressing into the muscles of his back, she could barricade herself, placing her feet on his calves with her shoulder protected and covered by his width.

Then she thought of the other boy. Young man. Whatever he was to the casual observer, he was not a man in the sense of this other bed occupant. Beardless, with muscles that were taut rather than bulky, with the skin down tight over thighs, bonier, lips drawn over smaller teeth that gave smaller kisses and felt smooth against the face. She felt like a child sleeping next to him, child's back against child's back, shoulders as small as her own, and hips that fit so neatly between her thighs that it was silly to put them elsewhere.

She wished for him as hard as she could, every emotional limb groping for a manifestation of this communal effort, heart, mind, cunt, all contracting to force out memories that might produce a reality.

Is it better to betray two people rather than just deceiving one? Doesn't that give everyone some kind of perverse equity? If she's betraying two men, then at least that means that she's thinking equally about them and, in a sense, betraying neither. But the lie no longer works. Not this morning.

Only a few days to go. Then she could at least speak to him. What was he doing now? Was he thinking of her? She prided herself on having learned, long ago, not to believe most of what men said to her. This knowledge did little, however, to produce any adaptive re-actions: all it did was to teach her to mistrust all she longed to hear. It did not teach her to stop asking for declarations, but it taught her to be wary of trespasses once they were made. Words were locked inside her own subconscious where she saw herself as betrayed or forgotten, and so she kept on demanding perpetual declarations, and kept mistrusting them.

So whenever she wondered whether the boy she really loved was thinking of her, she herded her thoughts like sheep back to this sleeping man who, as she knew from a thousand letters and repetitions and his willingness to sleep apart, was dreaming of her. She railed and simpered against any and all infidelities until he no longer looked at other women's breasts even out of curiosity. She regretted all that, as she surveyed him against the linear background. She wished that he would tell her of some gross crime against their relationship, tell her he was tired of her, mutter another name in his head-tossing. Only then would she be free of him. Convincing herself that she would take any such confession graciously, she tried to question him on his doings during their separation. But as his letters and phone calls asserted, he adopted the life of a monk with a shrine only to her (a candle surrounded by photographs of the two of them together, a lock of her hair, a poem she wrote) until they could be together again.

She tore at his fidelity like a cat fighting its way out of a sack, ripping, resenting, with the desire to destroy the enveloping enclosure and run like hell.

He stirred in his sleep. She moved over to his side and sat at the edge of the bed. He opened his eyes, looked at her face, dropped his eyes to her breasts and smiled like he was seeing two old friends. She leaned down and kissed him lightly on the forehead, and he clung to her until the clinging became a grasping and the grasp a hold. She felt a breathlessness—not from passion which was so soon departed, but from being held by such huge arms against such a huge frame.

She shut her eyes and gave herself up to the vivid remembrance of the boy's arms, his chest, and slowly undid herself from the entanglement of the man. He let her go, easily, but kept her face by drawing her eyes onto his glance. She refused to allow her eyes to drop, because she would then continue to be regarded like a statue or a painting, whether she sat beside him still or moved anywhere within his sight.

She could feel the panic beginning—the stirring horrible sensation, as if she had swallowed a bee and it was caught in her throat. She sat upright and clenched her fingers hard and shook her head at him with slow deliberate movements as articulate to him as any words ever were. He did not acknowledge her gestures but looked at her. He refused politely to adopt the currency of her unspoken despair. Why should he give her up?

✎ 62. *From my journal, 1978*

Freud wrote about the libido as tension, defined arousal as tension.
Maybe I have to exaggerate all emotional situations into a similar
state of tension to get myself prepared for that aspect of intercourse.

Why can't I just get laid?

✎ 63.

I left London in March of 1978 with less baggage than I'd brought,
and what I left behind was at least as important as what I took with
me. I've heard the same stories from nearly everyone who went on
a program enabling them to live elsewhere, even if that elsewhere
was Jersey City. You learn that you carry the ability to make a life
for yourself wherever you are. It is a lesson that should never be
underestimated; it is one of the few lessons on which we are all
tested again and again.

I spent the last two months in London however, indulging in sloth,
steeped and swimming in the waters of indolence. I look back on
that time and wonder whether I could have done anything differently. I doubt it. Maybe I was depressed. I couldn't make myself get
on with my work or get through the day without focusing on the
pointlessness of every single action.

Unhappily but profoundly in love, I was restless. I got close to my
British boyfriend only the way a cue stick gets close to a billiard
ball—prodding at, even moving, this completely impenetrable ob-
ject, something so self-contained it is barely affected.

I hunted through Camden Town flea-markets and thrift-shops for
things I didn't really need. I read trashy books and watched bad tel-

evision. The hardest things were falling asleep and waking up. I didn't want to lose the young man I was involved with and so I didn't bring up the fact that our relationship was eating away at my already rickety sense of self like termites at the foundation of a wooden shack. I drank rivers of tea. I drank shandies. I drank wine. I drank.

Rescue came with a letter from my brother. In response to the note of despair I'd sent him, he wrote simply, "You can always stop what you're doing." It was only one line written on the blue airmail stationery but it gave me all the permission I needed. I realized that I could stop doing nothing; I understood at that one astonishing moment that I could begin a voyage home that would also be a journey away from a shadowy life filled with compromises, inertia, and regret. I left town fast, not because the going got tough but because I knew that seductions of sameness were strong. I knew, too, that I'd used up my slothful days and that I'd never give into indolence for any length of time again. That was the bargain I made with myself; living as fearlessly as possible was the price I would pay for escaping what had once laughingly seemed like an easy life.

I'd like to reclaim some of those days when I was twenty-one but they're lost to the long afternoons when I half-napped and looked down the street to see what possible use other people were making of the day. When I have a guilty feeling coming on, I find myself feeling worse about those months when I did nothing than I do about anything else I've actually done.

64.

The thin young man with the green eyes sat at the edge of the bed and wondered whether there was anything else to say. His clenched hand rested against his mouth and he was aware that his heart was beating hard. He didn't want to hurt her; he took deeper breaths to calm himself. The room was cold now, but he dismissed the idea of getting up to put on a sweater. He didn't think it would be right, somehow, to move until they had spoken.

The girl lay with her face to the wall, every muscle pulling her features tight. Her hand was also clenched and pressed hard against her teeth, hurting her lip. With her other hand she traced the pattern of a circle on the white wall, over and over again. Some impersonal part of her mind noted this action, and surprised by the regular motion, she stopped.

The boy looked away and began to speak.

"I think it would be best if we split up for a while." He cleared his throat but did not turn around. The girl began tracing circles again.

"If you leave your keys on my desk—" He broke off, listening to his own words. He wanted the keys but couldn't think of how to ask for them. "If you just leave them there, that would work." He turned to look at her back and wanted to shake her, pull her up by the shoulders, get her the hell out of the room. He did not believe that he should have to go, leave, even for an hour. If she had any self-respect, he thought, she would be the one who left. She should have been gone by now.

As if hearing this, the girl sat up and looked at him, dropping her hands to her side. "I'll return your keys, don't worry."

He got up. He moved around the room. He picked up a book from his desk and moved it to the one she had been using. Her pens and papers covered every inch. He recorded such incidents now, her leaving things about, and he resented them. He got angry often, and the small considerations that had made their life together possible no longer came as a matter of course. He counted up every kind act he committed, and marked them off against her tears, complaints, and sharp words. Now all he wanted were his keys back, and he reminded himself as he walked over to her desk that she had never asked him whether she could have them copied in the first place. She had taken his key-ring one day when he was asleep and had copies made. He was delighted at the time and looked forward to her surprise visits. These thoughts skimmed the top-most surface of his mind and then skidded off.

He noticed that she'd finally stood up. "I paid for these keys," she said with no emotion.

He was furious and instantly frightened by the intensity of his anger. She watched his face darken and was also frightened, despite a sudden flash of satisfaction at having made him react.

"I'll send you money." He spoke slowly, like talking to an idiot or a child. "Now please just go."

She moved around him carefully, taking her coat from the closet, removing the keys from her pocket and throwing them on the bed next to where he sat. She put her hand on her mouth again. "You're going to miss me."

"So you've said." He waited and spoke again. "Go now before you say anything else, all right?"

"Fine." The girl looked around the room where she had lived, on and off, for two years. She had painted the room less than a year ago, stretching the paint as far as it would go, painting the wood-work near the ceiling, standing on a high ladder. She could still see five or six inches in one corner of the room where the old paint, yellow, sickly, was left uncovered. They had run out of paint and missed that small spot, but it wasn't important. He had held the ladder as she painted.

She closed the door behind her, afraid still to either leave it open or slam it shut. The boy watched her go, and heard the front door close. He walked across the room and put on a sweater.

65. *Conversations*

Liz to her new boyfriend: "So what if I slept with a couple of guys within the space of a couple of months? If I were male, they'd think I was a stud. But because I'm female they think I should be wearing a tube top with glitter saying 'I'm the Whore of Babylon.'"

To which he replies, "Which means I should have a T-shirt saying 'I'm Dating the Whore of Babylon and all I got was this lousy T-shirt.'"

66. *1978*

It is senior year, my last semester. I miss my boyfriend in England and I spend a lot of time alone in my single dorm room, still in Brown Hall. Iris lives on another floor and we see each other often but it isn't the same. My thoughts are in the air, across the ocean. I walk to my mailbox maybe three times day just in case a letter might have been mistakenly overlooked. There is a greater likehood of my seeing *the face of Jesus* in a *potato* than of my *overlooking* a letter, but never mind.

It becomes impossible to live this way, to keep my twenty-one-year-old self incarcerated in a narrow cinderblock room and my heart in a mailbox. One night I go to a poetry reading.

I'd seen the visiting writer at Sanborn House having tea.

Curly dark hair, flannel shirt, maybe thirty or thirty-five, a large man, wire-rim glasses, and eyes that caught my look and smiled. But he was talking to professors about publishers, so what could I say?

I go to the reading dressed and perfumed in predatory preparation, intent on his attention. I had looked at myself over and over again in the mirror at the end of the hall. I had grinned at myself and turned around to grin again: beige small sweater, light beige skirt, black boots (with soles so thin I could feel pebbles beneath them). Violet is already there. I sit with her and we speak about London and leaving and bitch about Dartmouth, sitting on comfortable chairs in the back of the room in Sanborn.

Looking and looking and looking at him, trying to smile like a beacon (please sir, read in this direction, look at me, I look pretty tonight). Vi and I sit there, listening to the erotic poetry, aware of my own cunt, his potentially hard prick making my eyes bedrooms (look at my mouth)—making such an effort to watch him around the heads of other people. He moves his chair, reads like an actor, and played a Chuck Berry song on this most unlikely, unwriterly guitar. I am listening—laughing out loud at the funny bits—and watching. Aware of myself and him.

The reading ends to applause. I say goodbye to Vi, go to say thank you to the poet.

"What's your name?"
"Gina Barreca."
"Isn't that a little ethnic for this college?"
(He said he'd gone to Harvard.)
"No more ethnic than talking about tattoos."

He'd read a poem about tattooing and the people around us laughed.

I go into the other room of the library, to the Resource Center where I tutor, my heart beating fast and between my legs, go to call Liz to make arrangements for picking up Iris at the train later. "What are you so excited about?" Liz asks. I decide not to tell.

Back to my room, maybe he'll call and ask me out. I gave him my name. Nobody else here by that name. I wanted it to be a summer night, I wanted it to be August, I wanted to scream, or fuck, or bite something, I wanted to do something. I called Tiger and told her.

"I saw this poet."
"*No poets,*" she said sleepily. She had been napping.
"He's not like a college kid, he's a real poet. He almost won the Prix de Rome and his play was just accepted by an off-Broadway company."
"Your ego is repairing itself, sweetie," Tiger yawns. "It's standing up on its hind legs and howling at the moon."

I walk up to Iris's room to use her phone and call the Inn but I hang up before it rings, giggling into Iris's pillow, feeling fourteen. I have to get outside. I have to *do* something. I walk toward the Hanover Inn and by accident meet Liz, so we go to the Bull's Eye for drinks. We talk about religion and sex and death but she has to leave and it's only just after 11. Too early for sleep. I call Tiger again who, when I ask if I can come over, mutters, "When you're a woman living alone, people think they can call you any time night or day. A woman living alone *is like the fire department,*" but she says yes. As I'm walking yet again past the Inn, I recognize the shirt at the desk and go inside.

"Hello."
"Hello."

"I was wondering whether I should leave a note asking you to go out for a drink."

"I *know* I should ask *you* out for one."

Walking toward the Bull's Eye again, close to a soft leather coat, sizing him up, maybe he's too old, maybe it was dumb, but exciting, oh exciting, he's asking questions to encourage me to talk.

Sitting at the Bull's Eye in the same place that Liz and I sat so soon before, speaking about prizes and men's colleges and he was drinking ginger ale and I am aware of his arms because he has his sleeves rolled up. Leaving, I tuck my arm into his—we walk, he laughs at some of the things I say, we walk in step—it is a lovely night—he slips his arm over my shoulder, I wonder whether I'd want to fuck him. I had taken my diaphragm out of its hiding place in my scarf drawer. We walk past the Inn. "Of course I meet you tonight of all nights," he says, eying the hotel with regret, "because I'm here with my sister and she's asleep upstairs." (It occurs to me only as I write this twenty-six years later that it might have been his wife, not his sister, asleep in that room. I ignored his wedding ring; did I also ignore a lie?)

We walk to where the new freshman class is building a bonfire. He's surprised that they are the class of '82. "Suddenly I feel very old," he shivers, half-joking. We look at the stars. He's cold—he holds my arms under him as we stand by the small fires dotting the Green. We walk to Fairchild, the glass and steel physics building, to warm up. "I'm incredibly cold," he keeps repeating, and then asks the real question: "Where's your room?" I am surprised by how unembarrassed he is of me—we walk around the pond and say hello when we see other people, other couples—we stop in front of Dick's House, I put my woolly red scarf around him, he puts both arms around me and we kiss. It was the only thing to do. But he slots his tongue into my mouth like he's serving me a subpoena. I don't mind exactly, but I do notice it.

We keep walking and laughing—we stop by the golf course, kiss again, wet, hot, tight kisses—and I feel his hard-on against me— we walk on, his glasses steaming up—back to my dorm, kissing— it's been a long time—yes it has—let's leave it at that, long being relative.

Going up to my room—it's a dorm room. I feel embarrassed in a way—he comes in, tells me it looks like his student digs back when he was in Cambridge, tells me stories about his student days, sitting in the only chair while I lie on the bed. He takes his shoes off, goes down the hall to the bathroom, comes back and lies beside me. I turn off the light, leaving the small one on my desk on—kissing— I don't know if I should let myself get excited—kissing—oh, it was sweet—wise face, he says I have, surprising and wise—he has a nice face, a lovely smile, but a body that does not live up to his poems. I feel guilty and ashamed for thinking this. But I know I didn't want to fuck—I ask him if I can undress him, but we both ended up undressing—what do we speak about? Other women. His girl-friend from college; a woman at work. He has curly hair and nice warm thighs, his cock stiff but not as pretty as the boy's in England.

As if hearing what I'm thinking, he asks me where my boyfriend is—he holds me—he tells me he was looking at me during the po-etry reading, that I had a face like sunshine in that room, that I wanted to be there for the words and not just for him—that I was pretty, that he liked my ass, singing the usual refrain and I was hop-ing for other words, saying that he wanted to put himself into me but I didn't want that, not him actually inside me, so I took him into my mouth to shut him up. He liked it and loved that he liked it, he kept stopping himself from coming, bragging a little, I'd like it if I only gave him a chance—yes, well, I'd be feeling bad about it now, so no—he held me, held me, kissed me all over, looking up once and saying "you have one of the great minds of America be-tween your legs" and I giggle but think that it's not actually true and he says, when we're done, "what a wonderful thing that we enjoyed each other." I expected something more from a poet.

Around 4 A.M. I walk him home and we keep kissing. At least there's still his good mouth, soft lips, even if what I was hoping to hear never came out of them. I don't even know what I was waiting for. "You should see my play," he says. He asks me to breakfast, but I say no. (Maybe it *was* his sister upstairs at the Inn.) He strips off the sweater I loaned him and, laughing, keeps kissing me goodnight all the while. He puts his cold hands on my red cheeks, which are warm from all the kissing.

I go back to the dorm. My room smells like a man and my mouth tastes of semen and myself. I sleep better that night than I have in weeks. I skip my morning classes, which I almost never do. I don't check the mail that morning.

I see him again as he's leaving campus. He's tired but runs up to give me a hug before his driver arrives. He is standing with a professor from the Russian department who he'd known in college, and I feel a little shy, but he brings me over and introduces me. I'm nervous about what he'll say, terrified of innuendo, but all he does is pronounce my name correctly, for which I am grateful, and explain that I was at the reading last night. It sounds legit.

 67.

I'd racked up classes in astronomy, Greek mythology, geology, film history, and finally, religion, in addition to every English class they offered. I saved comparative religion, as a treat, for last; it was Iris's major and I wanted, finally, the luxury of better understanding what she was talking about. I loved it. I had thought the most fascinating thing somebody could do was get in front of a room and talk about literature; turns out it's sexier to talk about life, death, hell, heaven, and the idea of a god. Who knew? Apart from Iris, of course, who started with *Paradise Lost* and ended up finding her way through this place and realizing that paradise was never actually *lost*—it had simply been *misplaced.*

68. *Conversations*

"He accused me of not experimenting when it comes to food," complains Vi, who rented a house with her boyfriend for senior year. "Experiment with food? I'll put a *Cornish game hen under his pillow.* I'll put *broccoli* in his shoes. I'd put *turkey* in his underpants only that might be *redundant.*"

It is the first argument from any of my friends that has at its core domestic issues. It makes her sound older, more settled. I am envious and uneasy at the same time, even as I laugh along.

69. *From my journal, 1978*

I keep writing the dates of times that should be far into the future. I am getting accustomed to the idea of leaving—at times it seems to be the only thing to do but then, as the reality of it approaches, I begin to feel as wary as when I could not conceive of leaving at all, through distance from the event and fear of the consequences. What looks like distance draws near and consequences fall into inevitabilities. I am tortured by visions of trying to recapture everything I've felt here— knowing that this is all so very important. To me, only to me, but important nevertheless. Keeping that in mind, I promise myself I can always rectify any terrible error. I tell myself this whether or not it is true.

The whole adaptive thing I'm trying to get straight in my head is my need to live in two worlds and betray neither—to be a fake in neither world. I keep thinking of double helixes: the idea of two matching but separate chains holding, pulling together but then splitting to replicate themselves, like people or problems or ideas. Joined at one point then parting to put together, gather individual partners. I put as much sincere belief in Greek mythology as I do in those science courses I took, but I can't believe either one is a genuine fact. Neither is as real as a toothache. There is no fact separate from belief. It was just as much a fact for people to believe the sun revolves around the earth as it is to believe that the earth revolved around the sun. Of course the world is flat—look around. What does the view from a spaceship mean? A "discovery," like a "cure," is a puzzle well put together. Clever. Satisfying. But it's still alchemy. A toy. Luck.

When I was a kid, there were fortune-telling tools we crafted from slices of scrap paper. We produced at least six or eight origami-type configurations of sharply folded paper, with numbers on the outside and predictions hidden within. You used both hands, index finger and thumb moving together, then apart, like dancers from a Jane Austen novel. One of the girls (it always involved girls, boys restricted their hands to the use of pleasure not prediction) would call out a number, and the other girl would then read out the corresponding fortune. "You will live happily ever after," the scrawled text might read, or "Stop now! Only danger lies ahead!" would sound a warning. One, two, three, four, fingers and hands, together, apart and the future sealed. Irrevocable. Silly. True. Stupid. Loves me. Not.

If I had the nerve, I'd make one now. I wish an older self could whisper to me what my fortune will be. I'd take even a hint, a glimpse. Happy. Not. Which?

This place, this world that existed for so long without me will close over and it will continue without me again. What was the line from that Merwin poem? "You grieve/ not that heaven does not exist/ but that it exists without you." I must get over the idea that any change is a negation. Love sure can be love even when it alteration finds. Anybody who looks back and believes that they made the wrong choice is a sentimental masochist or a self-indulgent jerk. Probably both. The real function of retrospection is to reassure the present, so how the hell can time be linked to the truth?

Getting through my time here required a great deal of courage. I do not know if I would have enough courage to do such a thing now, or again, for all my earned wisdom.

✖ 70. *December, 1978*

Not one for the grand gesture, what I remember best about my very last days on campus was drinking cupfuls of Tia Maria at noon in a friend's room after I'd just slipped my last paper under a mean professor's door. Make no mistake: this is not a memory I cherish.

But there I was, stretched out on my kindly, indulgent pal's floor, listening to Meat Loaf's "Bat Out of Hell" and thinking, hey, *I'm almost outta here.* This was in December of my senior year. If there were others in my class also leaving Hanover for good that cold bleak winter of what was still 1978, I didn't know them. There must have been others, it occurs to me now, but when I look back on that time it is so completely associated with isolation that it remains hard for me to think anyone could have passed through the same experience. Who else would have forfeited the fireworks and whistles signaling the end to a crucially important time of life? What other family would have allowed their kid to slip silently out of that world without any demarcation or distinction?

It was nobody else's business, believe me, that I left when I did. And it would be classier to say that I left because of a lofty issue, in protest over ideology, or because graduate schools just wouldn't hear of waiting another term of going on without me. But I chose to graduate early for reasons nearly unclear to me now, involving financial and emotional deprivation, involving a growing sense of uneasiness at life in a small town and the knowledge that I was no more a man of Dartmouth after three years than I had been in 1975. In retrospect, the time resembled nothing so much as the ending to an uncomfortable marriage made in one's first youth; an old joke involves one old friend saying to another, "Harry, I hear you're getting a divorce. Why?" to which Harry answers smilingly, "Because I can." Mostly I left because I could and there seemed to be few reasons to stay. For years it was something I didn't think about much. It has become something I now regret.

Leaving anywhere is tough. Maybe everybody knew but me; if there was a memo that went out to all of us at eighteen declaring this, I threw mine away without looking at it. I thought I was impervious to departure. I thought that it would never matter that I hadn't gone to a college graduation. After all, I pretty much erased the high school version of this, which involved appearing on stage with the thousand other kids from my class for about three minutes. We looked like extras from an old Cecil B. DeMille movie.

The one photograph my father took after the ceremony unfortunately positioned me directly in front of a sign blaring "No Parking Anytime." Maybe if the sign were in Latin it would have looked more like a graduation and less like Halloween, but standing in a white rayon rented gown, I looked like a cross between a very fallen angel on a bad hair day and a Klansman. So what could I be missing by not sticking around Hanover for two terms, paying what didn't need paying for? Friends, good friends who continue to be the best thing about my years at college, even then suggested I stay, that I find a job, that—at the very least—I return from wherever I was to attend graduation in June. Faculty members who had been protective and generous and kind also said that maybe I shouldn't be so in love with final exits, shouldn't get so hooked on the smoke of burning bridges. They were right, but I couldn't see that, blinded as I was by my own shortsightedness.

The decision to leave made every difference in those last three months. One of the things I could never get used to in Hanover was hearing adults say in perfectly serious voices, "Let's go to the Hop," because I always added, silently, the bass singer's follow-up on the 1950's record: "Oh baby." But that last winter I remember sitting by a fire in the Hop while somebody played the piano. Struck by a sense of how inviting it was, I realized, for the first time, that I hadn't accepted the invitation. And I thought it was too late to do anything about it.

I had a similar sense when having tea and cookies at Sanborn House one November afternoon after spending several dusty hours in the stacks. One of my cousins, hearing that I was at college and working part-time at the writing center to earn my keep, commented with a wry smile that my days involved "no heavy lifting," and I thought about his remark as I folded my hands around the warm cup of Constant Comment and watched the steam stealing all the heat. As lives went, this was pretty privileged. For my three years at Dartmouth I had been struck with a sense of being unwelcome, but how much more welcome I felt now that I was leaving. In December, I took the bus back to New York for the last time, vowing like Scarlett O'Hara with her fist to the sky, that I would never take a long bus ride again.

I went back to England on a one-way ticket. I found a job, moved in once again with my British boyfriend, and applied to a woman's college at Cambridge University. I didn't have any idea what I would do with my life. I hated when anybody asked what I was going to "do" with my major in English; they talked about my education the way you'd talk about a crazy old relative. But I was back in England, which is where my blind and hungry heart wanted to be; I was there for all the wrong reasons, but at least I was there.

In 1979, when June came to Gower Street in London, Hanover was once again another planet. My friends back home sent letters describing their plans for the big weekend and I admit to feeling a gut-level sense of envy. For many it was a big family event, becoming the most recent Dartmouth graduate in a long line of brothers, fathers, uncles, and grandfathers. For others from neighborhoods more like mine, it was still a big day, maybe bigger: it was the world's acknowledgment that they had succeeded, that someone in the family had made good. My father wrote to ask me if I wanted to come back for the event but I declined his too-generous invitation. I couldn't justify the expense, I explained, but I was giving myself too much credit. Now I realize that I must have also been afraid to go back because I already suspected that I had cut my losses too soon, and that I had taken my vulnerabilities with me when I flew across the ocean clutching the stub of a one-way ticket.

Great things happened at graduation, I heard. Great laughter, great speeches, great good-byes and promises of future meetings. I could only half hear the stories because otherwise I would have been caught up in longing; I had made my bed, I thought, and should lie in it, even when offered the possibility of more congenial lodging. I said I wasn't going back. James Joyce's advocacy of silence, exile, and cunning came to mind and I figured I could manage the last two even if the first seemed impossible. But Dartmouth, venerable institution it is, can hardly match leaving Ireland and the Catholic Church; to ally myself with Joyce was disingenuous, a cover for my own fears and stubbornness. I was looking for excuses not to go back, and found many.

Until a few years ago.

My husband and I were dating in 1990, and he suggested that we stop in Hanover on our way to Montreal. Resisting the idea, I came up with excuses that he laughed aside, not out of disregard but because he heard them for the evasive and inconsistent excuses they were. I made him promise that we would leave if I had a sudden flashback and hit the ground at the sound of a fraternity song, but nothing like that happened.

It was summer and it was beautiful.

We were both English professors at the University of Connecticut and he seemed more frankly interested in Frost's time at Dartmouth than mine, which allowed me to catch my breath and catch up with the last eleven years. With his camera, he took all the pictures I never had from my legitimate time there: in front of Baker Library, in front of my old dorm, in front of Thayer pointing to where I had fallen. Looking at all the still-perfect athletic young students, my dark-haired New Jersey guy muttered, "You know, I feel like 'Dondi' at this place."

It was a graduation of sorts, this return, because I saw that I had falsely denied the effect—positive and negative—that Dartmouth had on my life. I learned that it was after all only polite, as a southern friend once pointed out, "to dance with the one that brung ya." It felt good to dance with my past. It felt even better to dance into the future with a man who sensed the importance of bringing me back.

My first return to Dartmouth in twelve years, 1990.

🐝 71. 2004

When I dream about the place, which is more often than I care to admit, it doesn't look as it did in 1975 at the beginning or as it did in 1978 when I left for good. It looks like a film set, or a toy town you put under a tree at Christmas, one of the ones with fake lights glimmering through yellow cellophane windows. Students drift by, tall and blond, wearing down vests and knit caps.

The dream has no sound. Hanover is covered in snow. There is a mauve sky from a late afternoon in November, with the sun glowing just beneath black tree branches like a coal beneath kindling. I am headed toward Sanborn House, the English Department library where windows flicker amber and topaz. Sanborn House is home. I know that inside Iris, Tiger, Vi, and the others are having cookies. My walk across the Green, now as white and grey as concrete, is endless; I move over snow as in other dreams I move through water, weighed down and sinking. My heart beats hard as fast as a hummingbird's wings.

And I keep going.